SOFTWARE ENGINEERING

Academic Press Rapid Manuscript Reproduction

Proceedings of the Software Engineering Workshop
held in Albany, Troy, and Schenectady, New York,
from May 30 - June 1, 1979.

SOFTWARE ENGINEERING

Edited by

HERBERT FREEMAN

Electrical and Systems Engineering Department
Rensselaer Polytechnic Institute
Troy, New York

PHILIP M. LEWIS II

Computer Science Branch
General Electric Research and Development Center
Schenectady, New York

ACADEMIC PRESS, INC.

(Harcourt Brace Jovanovich, Publishers)

Orlando   San Diego   San Francisco   New York
London   Toronto   Montreal   Sydney   Tokyo

ACADEMIC PRESS, INC.
Orlando, Florida 32887

United Kingdom Edition published by
ACADEMIC PRESS, INC. (LONDON) LTD.
24/28 Oval Road, London NW1 7DX
Library of Congress Cataloging in Publication Data
Main entry under title:

Software engineering.

Proceedings of a workshop held May 30–June 1, 1979,
sponsored by General Research and Development Center,
the Rensselaer Polytechnic Institute, and the National
Science Foundation.

Includes index.
1. Electronic digital computers—Programming Con-
gresses. I. Freeman, Herbert. II. Lewis, Philip M.,
DATE III. General Electric Company. Research and
Development Center. IV. Rensselaer Polytechnic Insti-
tute, Troy, N.Y. V. United States. National Science
Foundation.
QA76.6.S6173 001.64'2 80-23025
ISBN 0-12-267160-0
PRINTED IN THE UNITED STATES OF AMERICA

84 85 86 87 9 8 7 6 5 4 3 2

CONTENTS

v

CONTRIBUTORS

Numbers in parentheses indicate the pages on which authors' contributions begin.

F. L. Bauer (1), Institut für Informatik der Technischen Universität München, Federal Republic of Germany

L. A. Belady (25), IBM T. J. Watson Research Center, Yorktown Heights, New York

Barry W. Boehm (37), TRW Inc., Redondo Beach, California

James M. Boyle (75), Applied Mathematics Division, Argonne National Laboratory, Argonne, Illinois

Edsger W. Dijkstra (95), Burroughs, Nuenen, The Netherlands

M. David Freedman (111), Bendix Engineering Development Center, Southfield, Michigan; and University of Michigan-Dearborn, Dearborn, Michigan

Peter Freeman (121), University of California, Irvine, California

Carl Hewitt (133), Massachusetts Institute of Technology, Cambridge, Massachusetts

B. Leavenworth (25), IBM T.J. Watson Research Center, Yorktown Heights, New York

Douglas T. Ross (149), SofTech,Inc., Waltham, Massachusetts

Jean E. Sammet (181), Federal Systems Division, IBM Corporation, Bethesda, Maryland

D. Tsichritzis (195), Computer Systems Research Group, University of Toronto, Toronto, Canada

Earl C. Van Horn (209), Digital Equipment Corporation, Maynard, Massachusetts

John F. Wassenberg (227), Norden Systems, Norwalk, Connecticut

PREFACE

Software engineering—the art, science, and discipline of producing reliable software efficiently—is a national issue. The United States spent over 15 billion dollars on software last year. The cost of software is growing at over 15% a year, but the productivity of software implementors is increasing at less than 3% a year.

Unless we can learn to use the limited supply of software implementors more efficiently, we shall not be able to produce all the software we need over the next decade. And unless we can learn to produce software with fewer bugs, we shall be plagued with overwhelming maintenance and reliability problems as computers proliferate throughout our environment.

New technology is needed. Additional resources must be invested in software engineering research and development if we are to obtain the promised benefits of the "electronics revolution."

On May 30, 31 and June 1, 1979, a workshop was held in the Albany, Schenectady, Troy area of New York State to address these issues. The workshop was cosponsored by the General Electric Research and Development Center, the Rensselaer Polytechnic Institute, and the National Science Foundation and included many of the key contributors to the software engineering area.

An important goal of this workshop was to establish a dialogue between three of the groups that have an important stake in this new technology: The researchers who are actually creating the new technology; industrial and government managers who see the current problems every day, and who will be the eventual customers for the new technology; and funding agencies, mostly in government, who are supporting much of the current research.

Among the questions addressed at the workshop were: Are we moving in the right directions to develop the required new technology? What is the state of software engineering R&D? Does it address the right issues? What should be the directions and magnitude of software engineering R&D over the next five to ten years?

One of the more stimulating aspects of the workshop was the interaction between the researchers and managers as they debated these issues. Happily, at least some of these interchanges were reflected in the updated versions of the papers submitted for publication in these proceedings.

We hope that these papers communicate some of the intellectual excitement that was present at the actual conference. We can truthfully say that all of the attendees' views of the software engineering area were altered in some way by their attendance at the workshop.

We would like to thank a number of people who made this workshop possible: Stu Miller, Manager of the Automation and Control Laboratory of the General Electric Research and Development Center, Les Gerhart, Chairman, Department of Electrical and Systems Engineering Department, Rensselaer Polytechnic Institute, and Bruce Barnes and Bernie Chern of the National Science Foundation.

A TREND FOR THE NEXT 10 YEARS OF
SOFTWARE ENGINEERING

F. L. Bauer

Institut für Informatik
Der Technischen Universität München
Federal Republic of Germany

INTRODUCTION

The term *Software Engineering* is now 12 years old; *Computer Science* as a new scientific discipline is perhaps 20 years
old; both are based on the development of the modern computer
which is not more than 40 years old. The rapid buildup of the
computer industry, which in the U.S. alone now employs several
hundred thousand people, has fostered in the public a belief
in progress that has not been matched by a corresponding understanding of the technical problems that underlie the computer. Even the professionals have underrated the complexity
and perverseness of programming.

Let us take a look backward. In the very old days, in
1947, a symposium on "Large-Scale Digital Calculating Machinery" (the word computer was not yet used) was held at Harvard,
organized by Professor Howard Aiken and sponsored by the Navy
Department's Bureau of Ordnance; it was probably the first
public symposium on computers. At that meeting, Admiral C.
T. Joy (Rear Admiral, Commanding Officer, Naval Proving
Ground, Dahlgren, Va.) mentioned that a foreign brother admiral had told him: "Admiral, aren't you glad you are too old
to learn all about this modern Navy?". Admiral Joy continued

> although some of us may be too old to
> learn all about high-speed calculating
> machines, we can at least appreciate what

> they mean to the Navy in advancing our
> knowledge of the science of naval gun-
> nery.

That is how computers started, with applications to firing
tables, neutron diffusion, telecommunication, cryptography,
and buzz-bombs - or I should say with Aiken, von Neumann,
Stibitz, Turing, and Zuse.

When the seemingly paradoxical term "software engineering"
was used in 1967 in a provocative way with regard to the software crisis, Dijkstra said

> you may be right for blaming users for ask-
> ing for blue-sky equipment but if the manu-
> facturing community offers this with a
> straight face, then I can only say the
> whole business is based on one big fraud.

The situation has changed since then. The combination of
the words software and engineering is no longer considered
paradoxical. Nevertheless, technically only limited progress
has been made. We are now able to identify the sources of
our troubles, but in many cases we have nothing to offer but
good advice. We are in the situation of a physician who
keeps trying out different pills on his patient in the hope
that some will finally cure him. The fact is, the hard times
for Software Engineering are just beginning. Yet to develop
a *methodology* is our real hope.

It is a tremendous step from programming tricks via programming techniques to programming methodology. Many people
will have difficulties in radically changing their views and
habits. It is as in 1958, when Grace Hopper explained the
heavy use of English in COBOL or rather in its UNIVAC predecessor:

> I used to be a mathematics professor. At
> that time I found there were a certain
> number of students who could not learn
> mathematics. I then was charged with the
> job of making it easy for businessmen to
> use our computers. I found it was not a
> question of whether they could or could
> not learn mathematics but whether they
> would. ... They said 'Throw those symbols
> out --- I do not know what they mean, I
> have no time to learn symbols.' I suggest
> a reply to those who would like data

> processing people to use mathematical
> symbols that they first attempt to teach
> those symbols to a vice-president or a
> colonel or admiral. I assure you that
> I have tried it.

Certainly, vice-presidents do much better now, and colonels or admirals retire at the age of 55, fortunately. Time heals wounds caused by mathematical symbols as well as those caused by the verification of assertions. There is always hope. How high the odds are, however, against an improvement can be seen from the following, quoted by Dijkstra in his new book:

> In a recent educational text addressed to
> the PL/I programmer one can find the
> strong advice to avoid precedure calls as
> much as possible 'because they make the
> program so inefficient'. In view of the
> fact that the procedure is one of PL/I's
> main vehicles for expressing structure,
> this is a terrible advice, so terrible that
> I can hardly call the text in question
> 'educational'. If you are convinced of the
> usefulness of the procedure concept and are
> surrounded by implementations in which the
> overhead of the procedure mechanism imposes
> too great a penalty, then blame these in-
> adequate implementations instead of raising
> them to the level of standards!

I have related the foregoing story to stress the point that it has taken us a long time to arrive at our present state and that it will be a long time before we shall have genuine software engineering. My guess is that *this will not be fully accomplished in the next 10 years. It needs a "change of culture"*. What I expect for the next 10 years, however, is more work on formalization and that its importance will be better understood.

Indeed there is no way out: a chemist cannot work today without a quantum mechanics background, a classical engineer has to learn some mathematics, and a *future software engineer will have to learn what formalization is and how to work with it*.

I intend to show in this paper that:

> *Formalization is less difficult than might*
> *be expected. It opens the way to new tools.*
> *Finally, it leads to program transformation*
> *as a basic methodological technique for*
> *software engineering.*

Software engineering is still a challenge to fundamental
research in computer science. It is not enough, to be satisfied with what Hoare and Dijkstra have achieved. Further
work is needed, in particular in connection with complementary
issues. Jackson (1975) was quite successful in practice with
his grammatically based description of data structures.
Functional programming, a first example of which was given
by Backus (1978), offers advantages in the early stages of
program design. Parnas (1971) has shown new ways in the question of encapsulation. These examples, and many others, show
that it is necessary to lean on mathematical concepts and
methods.

THE SOFTWARE LIFECYCLE

The phases of project management, as usually stated
[Zelkovic (1977)], can be compared with the development of
insects:

>   egg - requirement analysis, leading to
>   specification
>   caterpillar - general design
>   cocoon - coding and testing
>   butterfly - 'maintenance' (evaluation)

The sharp transitions are by no means helpful; they imply
dangerous situations for the animal as well as for the program. Preferably, a uniform representation is used, with
the analogy

>   mammals - uniform specification, design,
>   development and evaluation process.

The latter allows us to consider the life cycle of a program
as a uniform formalization ("evolution"). Consolidating the
whole process also means transition to a continuous process
of program derivation. We shall now investigate this process
more closely.

THE PROBLEM SPECIFICATION PROCESS: FROM REQUIREMENT ANALYSIS
TO SPECIFICATIONS

Formalization is worthless if it is not done at the level
of problem specification; otherwise the final product, the
program, cannot be formally compared with the specifications
- we do not know what "correctness" means.   Even philosophers
know this.

Once we arrive at a formalized description of a problem
from which to develop a program, a clear interface exists
between the process of analyzing a real world problem (requirement analysis) and the process of writing a useful program (programming).   The interface is the formal specification.

Rutishauser once has told me the story that in the early
days of operating the ZUSE machine at Zurich, a man came and
asked him: "Can you calculate why it is too hot in my silo?".
Given any problem from the real world - civil engineering,
physics, architecture or what you want - if a computer is to
be helpful (which it often just cannot be), it needs a bio-
logical, chemical, physical, organizational, logical or otherwise formalized model.

The software engineer will only in rare cases be sufficiently familiar with the application that he can be of de-
cisive help in the modelling process.   Yet, he must communicate with the end-user.   In some cases previously designed
software can be used with, perhaps, minor modifications.   But
some problems, in particular new and big problems, cry for
hand-tailored treatment.   Then the user has to be introduced
to the techniques of formalization, and the software engineer
will have to extract from the user the essence of his problem
and cast it into a formal structure.   If problems with high
risks for humans - e.g., political or economical ones - are
to be dealt with, it will be essential that the user be able
to verify that the specification the software engineer has
drafted is the right one.   We have to educate the end-user
that *formalized specifications are not necessarily unreadable
and incomprehensible.*

FORMALIZED LANGUAGE

There is a common complaint that *a "normal human being" cannot read and understand formalized problem descriptions;* we have previously mentioned Grace Hopper's relevant story. There is a deep misunderstanding behind this opinion: formalization is mixed up with the use of a particular notation, say the one of formal logic, or, more precisely, that of first order predicate calculus. Yet it would be a grave injustice to the "man on the street" to assume that he cannot think logically: What he has not learned is the particular notation of logicians, which is nothing but a form of shorthand. To be clear: *formalized language is a sublanguage of the full natural language.*

The converse is not true: Poems do not (usually) fall into the class of formalized language - but even poets (most of them) can read formalized language. After all, formal logic (first order predicate calculus) is not contradictory to common sense. To show this, consider the following example:

Example:

Using the concept "string of something" for short "string", and the primitives, "tail of a string", "head of a string", "body of a string", "empty string" and "concatenation"*, and

---

It would be dangerous, to use a picture like the following:

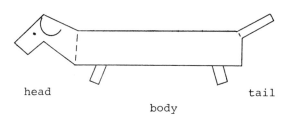

head   tail
                    body

to illustrate the abstract data type behind these primitives: the "empty dachshund" is a very tricky animal. Even the dachshund of length 1 is a misfit. A formal description is deferred to the section on Algebraic Data Types.

assuming that in the set of "something" a strict linear order
"is less than" is defined, we may give a specification of our
common understanding of the predicate "is sorted", applied to
a "string of something", in the following verbal but nevertheless formalized form.

```
< a string  s  is sorted
          if  s  equals the empty string:  yes
      else if the body of  s  equals the empty string:  yes
      else if there exists a string  u ,
                          a string  v  such that
          u  is not equal to the empty string
      and  v  is not equal to the empty string
      and  u  concatenated with  v  equals the string  s
      and  u  is sorted
      and  v  is sorted
      and the tail of  u  equals or is less than the head
                          of  v :  yes
      else:  no                                                    >
```

It requires no particular notational training to be able to
read this description and to check whether or not it corresponds to our intuitive understanding of the predicate.

A formalized shorthand version of the text may read:

```
Primitives:  body:   string → string
             tail:   string → char      (partial)
             head:   string → char      (partial)
             empty:  string
             &:      string & string → string
             <:      char x char → bool
```

```
Algorithm:
  issorted:  string → bool
  issorted(s)  ⇐  if  s  = empty then true
                  elsf  body(s)  = empty then true
                  elsf ∃ string  u ,  string  v :
                                  u  ≠ empty ∧
                                  v  ≠ empty ∧
```

$$u \ \& \ v = s \qquad \wedge$$
$$\text{issorted (u)} \ \wedge$$
$$\text{issorted (v)} \ \wedge$$
$$\text{tail (u)} \leq \text{head (v)} \ \underline{\text{then}} \ \underline{\text{true}}$$
$$\underline{\text{else}} \ \underline{\text{false}}.$$

We claim that every construct written formally in the first-order predicate calculus can be rewritten in "human" verbal form - after all, even logicians are not completely inhuman. Moreover, a recent trend (Montague) in linguistics deals with formalization of natural language; it may be interesting for the programming language specialist to study this work.[*] Formalization also opens a way to introduce new mental tools into software engineering.

NEW MENTAL TOOLS

"New" mental tools can be used to gain insight into the scientific background of the software life cycle:

o Non-determinism

o Existential quantifiers

o Algebraic Data Types
   (already mentioned by Wegbreit: "disassociate the meaning from the possibly underlying computational model"

o Functional programming

o Call by need

o Concurrent processes

In fact, these mental tools are not really new but they are not well enough known and used - they are unconventional. Perhaps the most surprising and philosophically most intriguing among these tools is non-determinism. We introduce it in connection with the specification of the above predicate *issorted*. A slight change in the text then gives:

---

[*] *R. Montague, Formal Philosophy. Selected Papers, ed. R. H. Thomason, New Haven-London 1974.*

```
< a string  s  is sorted
        if  s  equals the empty string:  yes
    else if the body of  s  equals the empty string:  yes
    else - let some string  u ,
             some string  v  be such that
           u  is not equal to the empty string
    and  v  is not equal to the empty string
    and  u  concatenated with  v  equals the string  s -
        if  u  is sorted
    and  v  is sorted
    and the tail of  u  equals or is less than the
        head of  v :  yes
    else:  no                                              >
```

The subtle difference means that an arbitrary choice of u
and v can be made provided it fulfills the first three conditions, u $\neq$ empty $\wedge$ v $\neq$ empty $\wedge$ u & v = s, and then
the chosen objects are subjected to the further conditions.
Accordingly there is then a new shorthand version:

```
issorted:  string → bool
issorted (s) ⇐.if  s = empty then true
                  elsf body (s) = empty then true
                  else let some string  u , some string  v :
                        u  ≠ empty ∧   v ≠ empty ∧
                                     u & v = s   ;
                      if issorted (u) ∧
                         issorted (v) ∧
                         tail (u) ≤ head (v) then true
                                            else false
```

Here we see a typical non-deterministic construct, the choice
operator "some" [Bernays (around 1930)].
    Because of its closeness to the existence quantifier, it
is called an existential operator.
    It can be shown that the non-deterministic version is
equivalent to the previous one; one only has to show that
in the third branch there always exists *at least one* pair u ,
v such that
    u $\neq$ empty $\wedge$ v $\neq$ empty $\wedge$ u & v = s .

This is guaranteed by the fact that neither s nor the body
of s is empty.

   The advantage of the non-deterministic version is that we
can immediately derive from it new versions - called *descen-*
dants by McCarthy (1962) - by narrowing or even specializing
the choice.

   For example, we may use for u the head of s (made into
a string) and for v the body of s .

   This gives after minor simplifications[*]

     < a string s is sorted
             if s equals the empty string: yes
           else if the body of s equals the empty string: yes
           else if the body of s is sorted
                   and the head of s equals
                       or is less than the head of the body of
                           s : yes
           else: no   >

or in formalized shorthand

     issorted: <u>string</u> → <u>bool</u>
     issorted (s) ⇐ <u>if</u> s = empty <u>then</u> <u>true</u>
                       <u>elsf</u> body (s) = empty <u>then</u> <u>true</u>
                       <u>elsf</u> issorted (body (s)) ∧
                             head (s) ≤ head (body (s)) <u>then</u> <u>true</u>
                                                     <u>else</u> <u>false</u>.

We may instead break s in two strings the length of which
do not differ by more than 1, or in some other way, and obtain
different deterministic, normal recursive algorithms.

A SORTING PROBLEM

   Based on the predicate *issorted*, a sorting problem can
now be formulated with the help of the choice operator:
< the result of sorting a character t in a string a which
   is sorted is

---

   [*] < *(the string made from) the head of s is sorted > is*
always true,
       < *the tail of (the string made from) the head of s >*
is the same as < the head of s >.

```
     some string  b  which is sorted such that
     there exists a string  u ,
                   a string  v  such that
       u  concatenated     with  v  equals  a
and  u  concatenated     with  t  made into a string
        concatenated     with  v  equals  b              >
```

or in shorthand,

```
   insort:  sortedstring x char → sortedstring
               where sortedstring = {string a : issorted (a)}

   insort   (a, t) ⇐ some sortedstring  b :
                              ∃ string u, string v :
                                u & v = a ∧
                                u & (t) & v = b
```

I claim that every one can understand this specification,
that is, everyone can check whether it corresponds to his
intuitive understanding of sorting. Note that *issorted* (a)
holds by definition. From this, *issorted* (u) and *issorted* (v)
can be proved. *Issorted* (b) then is the condition to be
obeyed.

In a few formal steps, we now arrive at a non-deterministic solution for the *sorting problem*:

```
   insort:  sortedstring x char → sortedstring
               where sortedstring = {string a : issorted (a)}
   insort (a, t) ⇐ if a = empty then (t)
                   else let some string u, char z, string v:
                               u & (z) & v = a  ;
                     if t ≤ z then insort (u, t) & (z) & v
                     ▯ t ≥ z then u & (z) & insort (v, t)
```

Again, descendants may be used to derive specific algorithms,
like linear sorting or binary sorting.

Linear sorting is obtained by using for u the empty
string, which makes z the head and v the body of a .
Insertion and trivial simplification then gives:

```
   insort (a, t)⇐ if  a = empty then (t)
                  else if  t ≤ head (a) then (t) & a
                       ▯ t ≥ head (a) then head (a) &
                                insort (body (a), t)
```

INTERMEDIATE NON-DETERMINISM

Non-determinism is not only helpful in connection with
non-algorithmic specifications, but can sometimes be used to
aid in algorithm development. The following problem which is
formulated without existential quantifiers specifies repeated
operations using recursion:

Primitives: o :   M X M → M

              -1 :   N → N (partial)

                where N : {1, 2, 3, ...} and others.

Algorithm:

pow: M X N → M

pow (a, n) ⇐ if n > 1 then a o pow (a, n - 1)

          ⫿ n = 1 then a

The description is algorithmically clear but does not give a
very efficient algorithm. It is better to derive from it
the non-deterministic version:

pow (a, n) ⇐   if n = 1 then a

              else if ∃ u, v ε N : u + v = n

                      then pow (a, n) o pow (a, v)

              ⫿ ∃ p, q ε N : p > 1 ∧ q > 1 ∧ p X q = n

                      then pow (pow (a, p), q)

which can be done if the associative law

    a o (b o c) = (a o b) o c

holds (thanks to the commutativity of + in N).

Although this algorithm is non-deterministic, it is nevertheless terminating and determinate. The third line contains
nested recursion, which in spite of its problems in execution
is not at all difficult to understand.

A descendant is, for example, obtained by choosing the
third line with q = 2 whenever this is possible, otherwise
choosing the second line with u = 1:

pow (a, n) ⇐ if n = 1 then a

              else

              if even (n) then   pow (a, n/2) ↑ 2

                      else a ○ pow (a, n - 1)

where a ↑ 2 is defined by pow (a, 2), i.e., by a º a
(common subexpressions)

One of the major advantages of non-determinism in programming
is shown here; it allows postponing design decisions while
carrying on the development until, in suitable circumstances,
the best use of the free choice can be made.

ALGEBRAIC DATA TYPES

We have implicitly used the concept of *Algebraic Data
Types*, when describing the primitives of the algorithms in
our examples. The "string of something" which was used in-
formally before has the following descriptive specification:[*]

type STRING(char) ≡ (string, empty, isempty, makestring,
                      head, body, &)

  empty : → string ,
  isempty : string → bool ,
  makestring : char → string ,
  head : {string s : ¬ isempty(s)} → char ,
  body : {string s : ¬ isempty(s)} → string ,
  & : string × string   string   ;

isempty(empty) ∧
¬isempty(makestring(c)) ∧
isempty(u & v) ⟺ (isempty(u) ∧ isempty(v)) ∧
head(makestring(c)) = c ∧
body(makestring(c)) = empty ∧
head(u & v) = if isempty(u) then head(v) else head(u) fi ∧
body(u & v) = if isempty(u) then body(v) else body(u) & v fi ∧
¬isempty(u) ⟹ (makestring(head(u)) & body(u) = u) ∧
u & empty = u

                                        endoftype

This formalized shorthand can be also expressed verbally.

The educational importance of this mental tool in the
software design process can not be overestimated. There is

---

[*]*For simplicity, we have omitted the operation "tail" and
its counterpart, which can be introduced conversely to "head"
and "body". Makestring(c) is synonymous with (c) above.*

the famous paper by Naur (1969) with the editing problem,
which was shown by Goodenough and Gerhard to be full of
blunders. The reason for the difficulty is that the problem
is logically much more complicated than Naur apparently realized. However, if a mapping is defined from a string of
something into a string of string of something, the way is
open to a fully rational specification and solution.

For the specification of Naur's editing problem, we introduce first an equality predicate on strings:

    equalstrings : <u>string</u> × <u>string</u> → <u>bool</u>
    equalstrings(s, t) ⇐ <u>if</u> isempty(s) ∨ isempty(t)
                       <u>then</u> isempty(s) ∧ isempty(t)
                <u>else</u> head(s) = head(t) ∧
                     equalstring(body(s), body(t)) <u>fi</u>

This allows us to specify a "substring relation"

    issubstring : <u>string</u> × <u>string</u> → <u>bool</u>
    issubstring(s, t) ⇐   ∃ string a , string z :
                    equalstrings(a & s & z, t)

For the representation of text, special symbols like "NL" for
new line or "BL" for blank are usually used. However, the
structure of a text is reflected more appropriately by a
string of words, where the words are strings of only characters. Let "convert" be a function converting strings of
characters and special symbols into strings of words; let
"equaltexts" be the equality predicate on strings of words
which can be based on "equalstring". Then the general editing problem is formally specified by:

    edit : <u>string</u> → <u>string</u>
    edit(s) ⇐ <u>some</u> <u>string</u> t : editform(t) ∧
                      equaltext(convert(s), convert(t))
where
    editform : <u>string</u> → <u>bool</u>

comprises the special requirements which should be fulfilled.
In Naur's case, these requirements can now be described as
follows:

editform (t):

(1)   No NL or BL is followed by NL or BL in t :

    $\neg$ issubstring ((NL) & (NL), t) $\wedge$

                $\neg$ issubstring ((NL) & (BL), t) $\wedge$

   $\neg$ issubstring ((BL) & (NL), t) $\wedge$

             $\neg$ issubstring ((BL) & (BL), t)

(2)   The non empty string t starts with a newline:

    isempty (t) $\vee$ head (t) = NL

(3)   No line contains more than max characters:

    $\forall$ string l: (issubstring (l, t) $\wedge$

         $\neg$ issubstring ((NL), l)) $\Rightarrow$

      length (l) $\leq$ max

(4)   Each complete line l is followed by a word w
      which is too long to be put into the line l with-
      out conflict with condition (3) :

    $\forall$ string l, string w: (issubstring ((NL) & l
      & (NL) & w & (BL), t) $\vee$ issubstring ((NL) &
      l & (NL) & w & (NL), t)) $\Rightarrow$ length (l & (BL)
      & w) > max

With such a rigorous specification, there can be no doubts
whether or not a given algorithm is correct.

FUNCTIONAL PROGRAMMING

Functional programming is another mental tool that in the
widest sense, should be used more often. Henderson and
Morris (1976) recently gave a treatment of the problem of
displaying all primes between 2 and N in "three lines" using
a function primesieve, which is hierarchically based on a
function multsieve, and can be applied to a sorted string of
natural numbers:

```
multsieve : natstring x nat → natstring
primesieve : natstring → natstring
multsieve (a, x) ⇐ if a = empty then a
            elsf x | head (a) then multsieve (body (a), x)
            else (head (a)) & multsieve (body (a), x)
primesieve (a) ⇐ if a = empty then a
            else head (a) & primesieve (multsieve
                      (body (a), head (a)))
```

Now primesieve(natinterval (2, N)), where

    natinterval: <u>nat</u> ˣ <u>nat</u> → <u>natstring</u>
    natinterval (i, k) ⇐ <u>if</u> i > k <u>then</u> empty
                       <u>else</u> (i) & natinterval (i + 1, k)

gives the desired string of primes. Again passive understanding of the algorithm, if read out from the symbolism, is immediate, although active formulation may need a bit more work.
This example shows that functional programming is a good
basis for specification. APL programmers know this - their
problem is that they have to go straight to a compiler.

    Compared with a usual program using nested loops, this
formulation is so much more transparent that Henderson and
Morris gave no "proof" for their system of recursion, assuming that it is obvious that it fulfills the specification:

   < the string of prime natural numbers between 2 and N,
    sorted in ascending order >.

But even a direct proof reads much simpler for the functional
notation than for the program with loops, despite the fact
that both programs cause - without regard for organizational
matters - the same course of action.

    How is this possible? The reason seems to be that recur-
sion does not have to be in the special form of tail recursion (which it is not in our example) in order to be easily
understood; however, tail recursion, which corresponds to the
performance of loops, is the most suitable form for execution
with today's machines. Indeed, even nested recursion, which
may be a nightmare to a programmer who should write an equivalent program with loops, is very easily understood.

    Functional programming in a more special sense uses func-
tions as arguments and results of algorithms. One of its
proponents is Backus (1978); it has to be stated, however,
that the practical possibilities of functional programming
reach far beyond the artificial fence Backus has erected by
the particular system he is using.

NON-TERMINATING ALGORITHMS AND INFINITE OBJECTS

Two additional examples of unorthodox tools are non-terminating algorithms and infinite objects. Since their theoretical handling is quite subtle, we do not attempt here to give more than a rough idea with the help of an example.

The algorithm

nats: <u>nat</u> → <u>natstring</u>
        nats (i) ⇐ (i) & nats (i + 1)

is such a non-terminating algorithm; it "produces" an infinite string of natural numbers in ascending order. The call

primesieve(nats(2))

correspondingly does not terminate, and at first sight the question comes up: What are infinite objects and non-terminating algorithms good for at all? The answer has been given by Henderson and Morris (1976). Essentially non-terminating algorithms may terminate in a special terminating environment provided the right sort of function call mechanism is used. Thus

head(body(body(body(primesieve(nats(2))))))

terminates if one uses the call mechanism that was discovered by Wadsworth (1971) ("call by need") and later in a related form by Vuillemin (1973) ("delay rule"). The catchwords indicate the basic idea: to postpone evaluation of an expression as long as possible. Under this call, only the first four prime numbers are calculated and 7 is the result.

Other examples of infinite objects are given by composite objects parts of which consist of the object itself, ring lists and doubly-linked lists being trivial examples. This new tool gives a fully new dimension to our algorithmic thinking and should be of great value for software design.

PROGRAM TRANSFORMATION

The trouble with building software comes from a mismatch. Programs which are intended to be effective on today's machines (even when so-called high-level programming languages

and a compiler are used) are rarely obvious, and obvious
problem specifications are rarely efficient programs - they
may not even be algorithmic.

Thus our main occupation is to convert a formalized problem specification into a program. If this is done according
to some (mechanizable) formal rules, it is called *program
transformation*. Of course, program transformation will in
practice be done step by step. Only small steps will guarantee that the effect of the transformation can be fully appre-
ciated; mastering complexity is the issue.

Within the strict functional level, transformations can
be based on two principles:

    (a)   modifications within the universal algebra of predi-
        cates of first-order logic including existential
        quantifiers;

    (b)   folding and unfolding of functions.

Moreover, algebraic laws in the algebra of terms may be
assumed to hold, thus allowing further transformations.

Such a core of a genuine applicative style (equivalent to
the λ-Calculus) is usually extended to include special shorthand notations for particularly frequent constructions, such
as notations for:

   o   alternatives (<u>if</u>-<u>then</u>-<u>else</u>-<u>if</u>) and guarded expressions
      in the sense of Dijkstra

   o   the suppression of parameter ("non-local" parameter)
      and the subordination of functions (block structure)

   o   object declarations ("constant declaration").

There are defining transformations for the introduction of
these constructs, e.g., in the case of object declarations:

    <u>let</u> a = E <u>within</u> F_a

is equivalent [Landin (1966)] to the application of the function $\underline{\lambda}$ a·F_a to the expression E,

    $\underline{\lambda}$ a·F_a (E)

obtained by permuting F_a and E.

Practical considerations suggest a further extension to
procedural constructs. Defining transformations connect the

procedural level to the applicative core. For goto's and
jumps this was discovered by Gill (1965) - they are nothing
but calls of (parameterfree) functions in tail recursion.
Used in this "decent" way, they are by no means harmful. That
variables can be introduced by defining transformations was
shown by Pepper in his recent thesis; assignments are obtained
from declarations with a re-used identifier. Equivalence of
this semantics has been shown. Pointers can also be introduced by a defining transformation which makes function application explicit [Bauer (1978)]; this subject will be
treated in a forthcoming thesis by Möller. How sequentiali-
zation and parallelization on the procedural level is connected to the applicative formalism has been studied in a
thesis Broy has submitted. Many other constructs of more or
less importance which make the playground of programming
language inventions so colorful, can be treated this way provided they are sound enough to survive the severe requirements of a transformational definition.

Formally, a program transformation rule is a pair of
program schemes ($\underline{D}$, $\underline{P}$) together with a condition $\underline{R}$. We may
write

$$\frac{\underline{D}}{\underline{P}} \diagdown\!\!\!\diagup \underline{R}$$

for such a transformation.

The application of a transformation rule to a program or
program scheme D means to find some interpretation of $\underline{D}$ which
gives D; the same interpretation of $\underline{P}$ then gives the result
P of the transformation. Sometimes, there is no interpretation possible (the transformation is not applicable); sometimes there are several. An interpretation is performed in
terms of some primitive object sets and operations defined by
an algebraic type A.

Many compact transformations are only valid under certain
restrictions R. To demonstrate their applicability it has
to be proved that the restrictive properties hold for the
algebraic type in question. Let I_A be some interpretation

over an algebraic type A. If R can be derived in A, then
the program or program scheme $I_A(\underline{P})$ is equivalent to $I_A(\underline{D})$.

It is also possible to have for $\underline{D}$ and $\underline{P}$ two different but
equivalent algebraic types A' , A'' (change of data type).

We now see that the process of building software also fits
in this frame: Given a problem specification $\underline{D}$ over an
algebraic type A' , an equivalent program $\underline{P}$ over an algebraic
type A'' is to be constructed. In this situation, A'' is
normally fully determined by the characteristics of the target machine or compiler. Any "solution" $\underline{P}$ over A'' for the
specification $\underline{D}$ over A' is the result of a transformation
scheme. The net result of a software building process thus
amounts to the addition of a new transformation scheme to a
thesaurus of those which are already in use in a given environment.

PROGRAM MANIPULATION

Program transformations based on the applicative core
mentioned above can be executed mechanically. If (notational)
extensions of the core language are introduced by means of
defining transformations, this possibility carries over.

In order to be free of purely representational considerations, we prefer to think of the core language (and its
extensions) as just a particular abstract data type CORE, the
terms of which, under the laws, form congruence classes corresponding to the usual syntactical classes.

It is common practice to begin with a change of type:
tree structures of the kind Knuth has called Lists (with
capital L) are powerful enough to implement the abstract data
type CORE. Rosen's technique for the application of a transformation can be specified in this implementation. The
complete specification including the abstract type of Lists
and the specification of the transformation process can be
done on two pages.

THE PROJECT CIP (MUNICH)

The program manipulation system (CIP-S) and the abstract
core language together with its extensions (CIP-L) are part
of a research project carried out at the Technical University
of Munich in the Research Unit 49, Software Engineering. This
project provides the background for the considerations of this
article. CIP-L is a "wide-spectrum language" which extends
outside, say PASCAL, on both ends; it is a "scheme language"
without fixed data types (apart from predicate calculus); it
is an "abstract language" which allows many representations.
In particular, dialects such as an ALGOL-like dialect and a
PASCAL-like dialect will be specified for the user's conven-
ience. Other dialects, say, a LISP-like one or one close to
the ADA language can be specified provided someone is willing
to write the corresponding string-to-tree and tree-to-string
parsers. Preliminary information on CIP-L was given in
SIGPLAN Notices, December 1978. With the bootstrap help of
a pilot model, a first working version of the manipulation
system will be implemented on the CYBER 175 at the Leibniz
Computing Center in Munich. The instructional and educational
aspects of the project have influenced a textbook "Algorithmic
Language and Program Development" which is to appear soon.

CONCLUDING REMARKS ON THREE COMMON OBJECTIONS

At first sight, several objections can be made to the
philosophy of software engineering as outlined here.
   (1) Imprecise and fuzzy specification - How does one
        formalize them?
   (2) Complexity - How does one cope with it?
   (3) Blind alleys and locked doors in the design-process
        - How does one circumvent them?
It is in the nature of the subject that no algorithm but only
good advice can be given on how to overcome these objections.
   With respect to item (1), if faced with an imprecise or
fuzzy specification, or if a precise and clear specification
cannot be given,

o Improve your formal abilities
o Understand your problem better
o Check whether you have "forgotten" some assumptions
o Check whether the *problem* is underdetermined
o Check whether the problem allows several interpretations in terms of models for algebraic data types
o Keep in mind that the programmer (rather than the
   problem) is more likely to be imprecise and fuzzy.

With respect to item (2), if the problem seems to be
rather complex, and if the previous advice has been followed,

o Decompose the problem in a formal way into sub-prob-
   lems
o Reduce the problem to its essence - it may then be
   easier to find a proper decomposition.

Structuring the problem is half way toward solving it. If
a problem cannot be decomposed (hierarchically and/or collat-
erally) into problems of the size of "simple exercises", no
rational treatment of the problem can honestly be expected.

As to item (3),

o Try again, try harder. There is no substitute for
   experience.
o If you believe in finding a solution, sooner or later
   you will find one.

REFERENCES

Backus, J. (1978). Can programming be liberated from the
     von Neumann style? A functional style and its algebra
     of programs, *Comm. ACM 21(8)*, 613-641.
Bauer, F. L. (1979). Detailization and lazy evaluation,
     infinite objects and pointer representation, *In:* "Program
     Construction" (F. L. Bauer and M. Broy, eds.), Lecture
     Notes of the International Summer School in Program Con-
     struction, Marktoberdorf 1978. Lecture Notes in Computer
     Science 69, Berlin-Heidelberg-New York, Springer, 406-420.
Gill, S. (October 1965). Automatic computing: Its problems
     and prizes, *Computer J. 8(3)*, 177-189.

Henderson, P., and J. H. Morris (January 1976). A lazy
    evaluator, *Conf. Record, Third ACM Symp. on Principles
    of Prog. Languages*, Atlanta, 95-103.
Jackson, M. (1975). "Principles of Program Design," London,
    Academic Press.
McCarthy, J. (1963). Towards a mathematical science of
    computation, "Information Processing 1962," Amsterdam,
    North-Holland, 21-28.
Naur, P. (1969). Programming by action clusters, *BIT 9*,
    250-258.
Parnas, D. L. (April 1971). Sample specification for man
    machine interface, Presented at the NATO Advanced Study
    Institute on Graphics and Man Machine Interface,
    Erlangen.
Vuillemin, J. (1973). Correct and optimal implementation of
    recursion in a simple programming language, Rapport de
    recherche No. 24, Roquencourt.
Wadsworth, C. P. (1971). "Semantics and Pragmatics of the
    Lambda Calculus," Ph.D. Thesis, Oxford U.
Zelkovic, M. V. (1976). Perspectives on software engineering,
    Computing Surveys 10(2), 197-216.

PROGRAM MODIFIABILITY

L. A. Belady

B. Leavenworth

IBM T. J. Watson Research Center
Yorktown Heights, New York

THE PROGRAMMING PROBLEM

During the last decade a great deal has been written about
the *unpredictability* of programming [Brooks (1975); and
Goldberg (1973)]. It is indeed difficult to forecast the cost
and the schedule of a program development project. The resulting product is also full of surprises: it runs usually
slower than expected and it requires endless *maintenance*.
Operation is continually disrupted by errors which must be
removed. Even without errors, most programs must be adjusted
to reflect changes in hardware and in functional requirements.
And the larger the program, the larger the development and
maintenance organization, the greater the problem.

In spite of this apparent flux, programming methodologies
in the past considered programs as static artifacts. Work
concentrated on the *development* of correct programs which, by
assumption, presented no challenge beyond delivery to users:
after all, programs do not suffer physical wear as hardware
devices do. However, in the early 70's systematic studies of
large programs [Belady and Lehman (1976); and Lehman and Parr
(1976)] uncovered and established the *evolutionary* nature of
software, namely that programs are not static objects but
undergo continuous *modification* to cope with the everchanging
environment. That is, in addition to dynamic execution on a
machine, programs display dynamics of their own evolution and
growth while execution is at rest.

The program evolution studies also revealed the phenomenon of *structural aging*. This sounds rather surprising since
programs are non-tangible objects. Consider, however, a software system consisting of many modules -- program parts and
data structures. As the case studies indicated, during evolution the system becomes periodically modified such that, in
each period, roughly the same amount of change is introduced,
to repair error and add function. Modifications during a
period impact a fraction of the totality of modules while
leaving the others unchanged. All studies so far indicate
that a *consistently increasing fraction of modules becomes
impacted* under modification (Figure 1).

An older system will then require more modules to work
with than when it is young. This increasing dispersion of
changes into the system results in longer schedules and
greater expenses. In fact, every modification makes the next
one more difficult to perform. Structure deteriorates since
in practice each modification is a patch, done in a hurry.

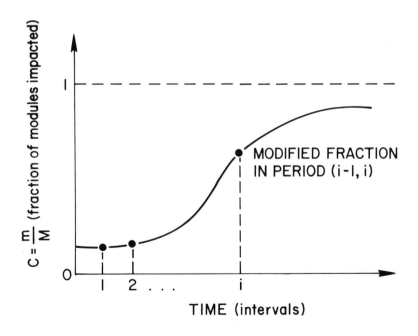

FIGURE 1. Structural Aging

Elegance, if any, in the original design is destroyed, and
new dependencies between modules are introduced which in turn
become conveyors of future changes. In the meantime the pool
of commercially available programs grows and so does, but much
faster, the modification demand. Recently it has been recognized that a growing majority of professional programmers is
involved in program maintenance, which in turn slows down the
spread of computer applications. It seems that the maintenance, or rather modification, problem is now the *central
issue of software engineering*.

Some progress has been made in productivity and program
quality by the acceptance of improved programming techniques
such as organized development, disciplined design and structured programming. The problem of constructing modifiable
programs is however a research issue at present. Focus is on
good design which keeps changes confined to small localities.
The greater the fraction of the program remains unchanged,
the more modifiability the design offers. It seems that techniques are needed which encourage the encapsulation of programs and data so that changes are localized. The most promising new concept which has been proposed and discussed by
leading software engineers for almost a decade is *data abstraction*. In the following pages we describe the relation of this
concept to program modifiability.

MODIFIABILITY AND DATA ABSTRACTION

The key to program modifiability is producing a program
such that changes to the program have only a localized effect.
It is this property of localization that we will emphasize.
Related to localization is the principle of "information hiding" [Parnas (1972)]. This principle is exemplified by a
black box which has a certain behavior and effects on the
environment but we do not know how these effects are accomplished. Since the workings of the black box are hidden from
the outside, it follows that any changes made internal to the
black box which *preserve* its behavioral properties will have
no adverse effect on the environment.

Subroutines which have no global variables satisfy the

above properties. That is, they hide their inner workings
from the outside world and localize the effects of changes.
The reason we prohibit global variables is that we want a
subroutine to have the same result whenever it is called with
the same inputs. If a subroutine has a global variable that
can be modified by another part of the program, then that
subroutine can possibly have different effects on the environment at different invocations. So the subroutine, if properly
used, can be an important structuring mechanism for producing
modifiable programs. But this is not sufficient - we do not
have comparable advantages in the realm of data.

The notion of abstraction is the key to information hiding and localization in the realm of data; in fact it has
started to permeate the whole area of "structured programming"
and its extensions. The idea of levels of abstraction pio-
neered by Dijkstra, Hoare, Wirth and others is another mani-
festation of this powerful concept. What is "abstraction"?
The best capsule definition we have found is due to Wegner
(1976) and says

> An abstraction of an object is a characterization
> of the object by a subset of its attributes ...
> If the attribute subset captures the "essential"
> attributes of the object, then the user need not
> be concerned with the object itself but only with
> the abstract attributes.

This prescription nicely fits our exposition of the subroutine
above where the black box exhibits the essential attributes of
a (process) object and we are unconcerned with the internal
workings of the object. As remarked by Dijkstra (1972),
"there is ... an abstraction involved in naming an operation
and using it on account of *what it does while completely dis-
regarding how it works*".

To show how the notion of abstraction also subsumes the
data realm, we must consider the notion of type. In the early
programming languages, not much attention was paid to type
(for example, in FORTRAN the basic types were integer and
floating point), and later, the conventional thinking was that
a type defined a set of values. The following is taken from
Hoare's (1972) discussion of types:

1. A type determines the class of values which may be assumed by a variable or expression.

2. Every value belongs to one and only one type.

3. The type of a value denoted by any constant, variable or expression may be deduced from its form or context, without any knowledge of its value as computed at run time.

4. Each operator expects operands of some fixed type and delivers a result of some fixed type.

5. The properties of the values of a type and of the primitive operations defined over them are specified by means of a set of axioms.

6. Type information is used in a high-level language both to prevent or detect meaningless constructions in a program, and to determine the method of representing and manipulating data on a computer.

The principle that Hoare is alluding to in Item 6 is that of strong type checking, which means that the type of every data object used in the program can be determined at compile time. This capability is especially valuable when the programmer is able to declare his own data types of which more will be said later.

The current view is that a type is a set of values *together* with a set of primitive operations. A number of ideas have led to the evolutionary development of the notion of data abstraction: the programming language SIMULA 67 [Myhrhaug and Nygaard (1970)], the additional work of Hoare (1972) on the relationship between abstract type and its concrete representation, the paper by Liskov and Zilles (1974), and the development of the programming languages CLU [Liskov, *et al.* (1977)] and ALPHARD [Wolf, *et al.* (1975)], among others, which exemplify abstraction mechanisms.

The currently acceptable view of data types fits the prescription of data abstraction as given above. Following the black box analogy, we not only hide the concrete representation of data objects inside the black box, but also the primitive operations on that representation. Furthermore, the programmer may only manipulate objects of some type by using the particular operations that have been defined for that type. These are the characteristic operations which determine the observed behavior by the outside world. Analogous to the subroutine black box, we are only interested in the behavior

of an object, and not how that behavior is carried out. This
means that internal representations and the implementation of
primitive operations can be changed as long as the behavioral
characteristics are preserved. Another important consequence
is that the inner workings of the black box cannot be changed
from the outside. Many of the problems in maintaining software are due to the fact that the concrete representations
of data structures are exposed to any and all programmers who
have a need to modify the program. This leads to a ripple or
cascading effect that has been written about [Belady and
Lehman (1976)].

While "structured programming" has been effective in sys-
tematizing and imposing discipline on the use of control
structures, it has had little to say about data structures.
An early awareness of this missing ingredient in structured
programming was articulated by Henderson and Snowdon (1972):

> The elaboration of requisite data structures
> should be as explicit as the elaboration of the
> sequence of operations in a program. A pro-
> gramming language should therefore provide fa-
> cilities for the conception of abstract data
> structures and their subsequent elaboration.

MODULES

We have already alluded to the notions of information
hiding and levels of abstraction. In what follows we will use
the term *module* to refer not only to a subroutine but also to
the implementation of a data abstraction. A module can be
invoked or referenced by any other module in a system, and
has the capability of being independently compiled.

Myers (1978) talks about the underpinning of a good design
and proposes three means of reducing complexity in any type of
system:

1. partitioning the system into parts having
   identifiable and understandable boundaries.

2. representing the system as a hierarchy.

3. maximizing the independence among the parts
   of the system.

The "parts" mentioned above clearly refer to the modules

of a system, and the goal of maximizing the independence among
the modules is equivalent to minimizing the overall intercon-
nectivity of the modules.

From the point of view of program modifiability, any system organization which minimizes the connections between the
parts must minimize the impact of any modifications made to
the system.

USE AND DEFINITION OF DATA ABSTRACTIONS

Let us consider a queue as an example of a data abstraction. A queue is defined as a "linear list for which all
insertions are made at one end of the list; all deletions
(and usually all accesses) are made at the other end" [Knuth
(1969)]. The characteristic first-in first-out property of
queues is shared with the corresponding FIFO method of pricing
inventories used by accountants. We will consider queues in
terms of the operations that characterize them; we will not
be concerned with their implementation. These operations are
basically creating a queue, adding an element at one end,
accessing or removing an element from the other end, and testing for the empty queue. Let us assume that we are dealing
with a queue of integers. Then the operations can be
expressed by the following rules or axioms:

```
        TYPE QUEUE
(1)   CREATE () -> QUEUE
(2)   ADD(QUEUE,INT) -> QUEUE
(3)   FRONT(QUEUE) -> INT
(4)   REMOVE(QUEUE) -> QUEUE
(5)   EMPTY(QUEUE) -> BOOL
```

Rule (1) says that when the CREATE operation is applied
(to no arguments), a queue is created. Rule (2) says that
adding an integer (INT) to a queue results in another queue.
Rule (3) says that the result of accessing the first element
of a queue is an integer. Rule (4) says that removing an element from a queue results in another queue. Finally, Rule
(5) defines the operation that allows us to test a queue for
the empty condition, where BOOL represents a Boolean (binary)
type which has two values: TRUE and FALSE. In writing a

program, we should be careful to test a queue for the empty
condition before performing a FRONT or REMOVE operation. In
some cases, it is difficult to say what constitutes a
"complete" set of operations on some data abstraction. For
example, for some applications, it might be necessary to add
a COUNT operation which would determine the number of elements
in a queue. Every abstraction has its own set of characteristic operations which are defined for the abstraction. Since
ADD and REMOVE are typical names that would be used to apply
to many other data types, it is useful to qualify the operation name with the name of the type when the operation is
invoked. Thus the following sequence of operations would
create a queue, add two integers to it, access the first element and then remove it.

                X = QUEUE · CREATE ();
                X = QUEUE · ADD(X,3);
                X = QUEUE · ADD(X,5);
                Y = QUEUE · FRONT(X);
                X = QUEUE · REMOVE(X);

     As indicated above, the user of the queue abstraction can
manipulate instances of queues by using the allowable operations; in fact he can use these operations and only these.
The user in most cases is *unaware of the internal representation* of the queue and the manner in which the operations act
on this representation. Even if the user knows how the
abstraction is implemented, he is unable to make use of this
knowledge because he is *prevented from gaining access* to
either the internal representation or the associated operations. We call the module which encapsulates both the internal representation and the operations a *capsule*. In
Myers' terminology [Meyers (1978)], a capsule is called an
Informational Strength Module.

     An application program is more amenable to change when
it is originally structured in terms of those abstractions
which are meaningful for that application. Furthermore, it
is less likely that a change will impact a program adversely
because of the locality of reference, and hiding of low level
details and data structures. In the same way that we distinguish between systems and applications programmers, it is

possible to make a distinction between two classes of programmers using data abstractions. One type of programmer will
be provided with a set of data abstractions which are appropriate for the application class of interest. This programmer will not be concerned with the implementation of the
abstractions. The second type of programmer will be trained
to define new abstractions; he will be in effect a "building
block" applications programmer.

TYPE GENERATORS

The idea of a queue can be generalized further. Instead
of just considering a queue of integers, we can talk about the
notion of a queue in general, that is, any queue of items
waiting for service. The items might be jobs to be executed
by an operating system, orders to be processed, or any kind
of work elements in general. Instead of defining a new kind
of queue for each individual frame of reference, it is possible to define a queue of type T, where T can be any other
legitimate type. The rules or axioms analogous to those
defined above would be:

```
        TYPE QUEUE [T:TYPE]
(1)   CREATE () -> QUEUE[T]
(2)   ADD(QUEUE[T],T) -> QUEUE[T]
(3)   FRONT(QUEUE[T]) -> T
(4)   REMOVE(QUEUE[T]) -> QUEUE[T]
(5)   EMPTY(QUEUE[T]) -> BOOL
```

A data abstraction that is parameterized in this way is
called a type generator. Once a type generator has been
defined in such a manner, it may be *customized for use in
different contexts*. We call this customizing process instantiation. The instantiation of the generalized queue to a
queue of integers, for example, would be realized by the reference QUEUE[INT].

THE PROGRAM MODIFIABILITY PROJECT

Data abstraction is not a new idea but it has not been
tried at the scale of commercial programs. This is because
software engineering is polarized around *two subcultures*: the
speculators and the doers. The former invent but do not go
beyond publishing novelty, hence never learn about the idea's
usefulness -- or the lack of it. The latter, not funded for
experimentation but for efficient product development, must
use proven, however antiquated, methods. Communication between them is sparse, and questions as "Does data abstraction
improve modifiability?" can be answered by neither.

In contrast, our project is *an experiment* to get results
which will help answer this question. For credibility -- both
technological and organizational -- we chose an existing program, which happens to be an operating system component of the
100K lines of code category, as an experimental vehicle. We
are *rewriting* the program *for modifiability*, at the same time
inventing and using a variety of tools to aid this process.
For example, *PL/I* has been extended by a *preprocessor* to
encourage the creation of data types. We also found a need
for, and then developed, new graphic techniques to make program structuring and restructuring efficient, and documentation automatic. We intend to transfer these tools to the community of software engineers.

An important aspect of reducing complexity is to fight the
"part number explosion" by designing around reusable and perhaps standard program parts. For example, queues of identical
behavior can be found all over in present day systems, yet the
queues are implemented slightly differently by the different
programmers involved. The standard use of an abstract *type*
generator called "queue" could drastically *simplify the de-*
sign. Similarly, in the performance area, encapsulation of
programs and data would facilitate a more systematic "tuning"
by permitting to test and compare alternative designs and algorithms in a real life executing environment -- hardly a
possibility today.

As the project concludes, we will *compare the old with the*
new, designed for modifiability, version. Times required

to perform a selected set of modifications will be measured.
We also plan to compare the depths of change penetration into
the two versions.   Experience as well as quantitative results
will be published afterwards.

REFERENCES

1. Belady, L. A., and Lehman, M. M. (1976).   A model of
    large program development, *IBM Systems Journal 15(3)*,
    225-252.
2. Brooks, Frederick P., Jr. (1975).   "The Mythical Man-
    Month," Essays on Software Engineering, Addison-Wesley
    Publishing Company.
3. Dijkstra, Edsger W. (1972).   Notes on structured program-
    ming, *In* "Structured Programming," Academic Press, New
    York.
4. Goldberg, J. (ed.) (September 1973).   "Proceedings of the
    Symposium on the *High Cost of Software*," Stanford Research
    Institute.
5. Henderson, P., and Snowdon, R. (1972).   An experiment in
    structured programming, *BIT 12*, 38-53.
6. Hoare, C. A. R. (1972).   Notes on data structuring, *In*
    "Structured Programming," Academic Press, New York.
7. Hoare, C. A. R. (1972).   Proof of correctness of data
    representations, *Acta Informatica*, 271-281.
8. Knuth, Donald E. (1969).   "The Art of Computer Program-
    ming," Vol. 1, Addison-Wesley, Reading, MA.
9. Lehman, M. M., and Parr, F. N. (Oct. 1976).   "Program
    Evolution and its Impact on Software Engineering," Pro-
    ceedings of the 2nd International Conference on Software
    Engineering, San Francisco, 350-357.
10. Liskov, B., and Zilles, S. (April 1974).   Programming
    with abstract data types, *SIGPLAN Notices 9(4)*, 50-59.
11. Liskov, B., *et al.* (Aug. 1977).   Abstraction mechanisms
    in CLU, *Communications of the ACM 20*, 564-576.
12. Myers, Glenford J. (1978).   "Composite/Structured Design,"
    Van Nostrand Reinhold, New York.
13. Myhrhaug, B., and Nygaard, K. (1970).   "The SIMULA 67
    Common Base Language," Norwegian Computing Center, Oslo.

14.   Parnas, D. L. (Dec. 1972). On the criteria to be used in
      decomposing systems into modules, *Communications of the
      ACM 15(12)*, 1053-1058.

15.   Wegner, Peter (December 1976). Programming languages --
      the first 25 years, *IEEE Transactions on Computers
      C-25(12)*.

16.   Wulf, W. A., *et al.* (1975). Abstraction and verification
      in Alphard, *In* "New Directions in Algorithmic Languages,"
      (S. A. Schuman, ed.), IRIA.

SOFTWARE ENGINEERING - AS IT IS

Barry W. Boehm

TRW Inc.

Redondo Beach, California

SUMMARY AND ABSTRACT

This paper presents a view of software engineering as it
is in 1979. It discusses current software engineering practice with respect to lessons learned in the past few years,
and concludes that the lessons are currently not heeded roughly half of the time. The paper discusses some of the factors
which may account for this lag, including rapid technological
change, education shortfalls, technology transfer inhibitions,
resistance to disciplined methods, inappropriate role models,
and a restricted view of software engineering.

The paper also updates a 1976 state of the art survey of
software engineering technology, including such topics as requirements and specifications, design, programming, verification and validation, maintenance, software psychology, and
software economics. It concludes that the field is making
solid progress, but that it is growing more complex at a
faster rate than we can put it in order.

SOME SOFTWARE ENGINEERING LESSONS LEARNED

Recently, I reviewed a paper which succinctly summarized
many of the software engineering lessons we have (hopefully)
learned over the past few years. Here are some excerpts:

1. Testable Requirements

"As soon as specifications for a system program are definitive, contractors should begin to consider how they will
verify the program's meeting of the specifications. In fact,
they should have had this in mind during the writing of the
specifications, for it is easy to write specifications in such
terms that conformance is impossible to demonstrate. For
example: 'The program shall satisfactorily process all input
traffic presented to it.'"

2. Precise Interface Specifications

"The exact interpretation of digital formats, the rise
and fall times of waveforms, special restrictions as to when
each type of data may or may not be sent - these and sundry
other details must be agreed on by all parties concerned and
clearly written down. Accomplishing this is apt to be a monu-
mental and tedious chore, but every sheet of accurate interface definition is, quite literally, worth its weight in
gold."

3. Early Planning and Specification

"If management takes the casual list-on-paper attitude
toward a computer program, the consequence will be procrasti-
nation of complete program specification, followed by dis-
belief and consternation when lack of a proper program delays
the whole system."

4. Lean Staffing in Early Phases

"The designers should not be saddled with the distracting
burden of keeping subordinates profitably occupied....Quantity
is no substitute for quality; it will only make matters
worse."

5. Care and Time Budgeting

"Budgets of time and storage, as mentioned earlier, should
be set up, and monthly or more frequent reports are advisable
on how well they are being adhered to....[For storage budgets,

include]... a safety factor of 25% or more, depending on the
estimator's self-confidence and the likelihood of expansion
in program requirements (they *always* expand)."

6.   *Careful Choice of Language*

    "Choosing a [Higher Order Language], like choosing a wife,
is hard to undo after getting involved, and is not to be taken
lightly."

7.   *Objective Progress Monitoring*

    "Percent-of-completion estimates will be asked for, and
unless tasks are defined with unusual care, figures will be
difficult to arrive at or decidedly misleading."

8.   *Defensive Programming*

    "Programmers should be imbued with the doctrine of anti-
cipating possible troubles and detecting or correcting them
[in their program]."

9.   *Integration Planning and Budgeting*

    "A common error in planning production of a program is to
underestimate the time needed to combine units after they
have been coded."

10.   *Early Test Planning*

    "Program acceptance tests should be defined early enough
for contemplated acceptance-test inputs to be used in the
terminal stages of program checkout."

HOW WELL HAVE THE LESSONS BEEN LEARNED?

    Let us compare the above lessons learned with some sam-
ples of current software engineering practice gathered from
a set of 50 term papers from a software engineering course I
gave at USC earlier this year. The examples are drawn from
recent government, industry, and university software projects
in the Los Angeles area, and should form a reasonably representative sample of "Software Engineering, As It Is" as seen

by the working-level software engineer.

1. *Testable Requirements*

"A requirements spec was generated. It had a number of untestable requirements, with phrases like 'appropriate response' all too common. The design review took weeks, yet still retained the untestable requirements."

"The only major piece of documentation written for the project was a so-called specification. Actually, the specification was written after the program was completed and looked more like a user's manual."

2. *Precise Interface Specifications*

"No one had kept proper control over interfaces, and the requirements specs were still inexact."

"The interface schematics were changed over the years and not updated, so when we interfaced with the lines, fuses were burned, lights went out...".

"The interface between the two programs was still not exact. When interfacing the two programs we ran into run time errors. Debugging was difficult because of the lack of documentation. We also began to forget exactly what our code did in certain situations and wished we had done more documentation."

3. *Early Planning and Specification*

"Despite one team member's efforts to develop a plan and some interface specs, the other two members felt there was no time or need to plan anything, and that each member should begin coding to complete the project on time. In fact, this did not save time, but caused many problems and delays."

"A software development plan was thrown together at the customer's request. It contained such good words as 'structured programming,' 'chief programmer team,' 'structured walkthroughs,' etc. This plan has been ignored since its creation both by the project manager and the software head."

"This is all common sense, yet I know of no R&D minicomputer installation that uses a formal documentation procedure.

It is with surprise that an engineer finds that paperwork can
actually save time."

4. *Lean Staffing in Early Phases*

"At an early stage in the design, I was made the project
manager and given three trainees to help out on the project.
My biggest mistake was to burn up half of my time and the
other senior designer's time trying to keep the trainees busy.
As a result, we left big holes in the design which killed us
in the end."

5. *Core and Time Budgeting*

"The core size is already three times the budget, and is
running over the 90% mark. Two-thirds of the program is running from slow memory, making the execution time well over
budget as well."

"This machine had a limited core size which resulted in
much trickery and use of machine-dependent techniques in
order to get the program to fit."

"Little planning was done, and the estimates of what the
software development would entail were arbitrarily cut by the
first project manager."

6. *Careful Choice of HOL*

"Although two other computer systems were clearly better
as a host for our upgrade, we were locked into Brand X because of the huge inventory of code we had written in a Brand
X-oriented HOL."

7. *Objective Progress Monitoring*

"Monthly status reports saying X% complete were given to
the customer. As predicted in the text, the 50% mark tended
to get reported as 90% complete."

8. Defensive Programming

"The programmer was a victim of the sad illusion that if
the users were given a set of rules for entering the data,
they would enter the data correctly. She had not even dreamed
of the things users could do to destroy the database."

"The program is not very guarded. In an effort to save
money, several types of error checking proposed were eliminated."

9. Integration Planning and Budgeting

"No integration plan has been constructed, nor have con-
figuration management procedures been established."

10. Early Test Planning

"The acceptance test was a disaster. The users got into
some of the exotic options and everything blew up. After
that, we had a hard time getting them to believe anything we
said about the system. There was no test planning - we just
rushed into it blind."

11. Software Standards: General

"The design was not in modules, making it impossible to
extend the use of the program. It was easier to write a new
program than modify or correct the existing one."

"Rather than attempt to restructure the particular area
that is being worked on, most of the programmers insert
"patches" that cause the flow of control to snake around so
that it is nearly impossible to try to follow the logic."

12. Software Management: General

"Morale dropped to such a low level that we were no longer
a team. Deadlines were not met, interfaces did not work,
programs did not fit requirements, and people quit."

To be fair, I should point out that the above excerpts
are not a fully representative sample of the project experiences cited in the term papers. There were about an equal

number of positive experiences in which people had evidently
learned the lessons identified above and applied them successfully.

HOW SOON WILL WE LEARN THESE SOFTWARE ENGINEERING LFSSONS?

Still, a 50% rate of applying these lessons is not very
acceptable. It would certainly appear that the paper quoted
above speaks directly to the current problems faced by software engineering practitioners. Its advice is timely, topi-
cal, and evidently much-needed today. It would appear, for
example, to be a good candidate for this book.

Unfortunately, the paper has already been published, in
1961. It is "Pitfalls and Safeguards in Real-Time Digital
Systems with Emphasis on Programming," by W. A. Hosier. It
appeared in the IRE Transactions on Engineering Management in
June 1961. It is based on the software engineering experiences accumulated on the U.S. SAGE and BMEWS command and control projects in the late 1950's. In the software engineering
field, I would recommend everyone reading it, for two main
reasons:

1. Although parts of the paper are a bit dated, most of
    its advice is still very good and well-expressed.
    (Perhaps the most striking anachronism in the world
    of 1979 is the statement that choosing a wife is hard
    to undo.)

2. I would hope that, in reading it, you would find your-
    self bothered, as I was, by the question: "If we knew
    all those things 18 years ago, why aren't we doing
    them now?"

I think this question is worth exploring, as its answers
are certainly relevant to the topic question: "How soon will
we learn these software engineering lessons?" In particular,
the next section will discuss some likely reasons why our
progress has been slow in assimilating software engineering
techniques, and suggest ways that we might be able to speed
up the process.

SOME FACTORS INHIBITING GENERAL PROGRESS IN SOFTWARE
ENGINEERING PRACTICE

Here are six factors which I believe are inhibiting our
general progress in software engineering practice:
1. The field is growing rapidly.
2. We aren't teaching many of the above lessons to
   students.
3. Technology transfer is slow.
4. We resist the required discipline.
5. We have our role models mixed up.
6. We often take a restricted view of software engineering.

1. The Field is Growing Rapidly

Our software engineering techniques have to be reexamined
every time we are confronted with a significant change in the
computer technology we work with. Although we generally find
(as with microprocessors) that the general principles of software engineering still apply [Rauscher (1978); and Magers
(1978)], we find that some techniques (e.g., instrumentation
and test techniques) need to be modified to fit the new technology. There is not much that we can or want to do to eliminate this source of problems.

The field is also growing rapidly in terms of the number
of people assimilated per year, who must necessarily relearn
many software engineering lessons for themselves. We should
be able to improve our status here via education, as discussed
below.

2. We Aren't Teaching Many of the Above Lessons to Students

A recent survey [Thayer, et al. (1979)] of software engineering instruction found large discrepancies between what
professors felt were critical software engineering issues and
what was being covered in software engineering courses. Of
20 major issues, only two (plan for maintainability and control quality) were covered to the extent commensurate with
the issue's criticality. The other 18 issues (e.g., plan

requirements, plan project, plan test, control visibility)
have a very high correlation with the issues discussed above,
but were under-covered in current courses.

The main reasons given for not covering those issues more
were:
- lack of expertise
- lack of texts and other teaching materials
- inappropriate for computer science departments
Hopefully, recognition of the first two reasons will lead to
activities to fill the needs expressed. The third reason was
given by some professors who felt that such management-
oriented material belonged in the business school. However,
none of the business schools were teaching such material,
either.

Our University education does best when it teaches people
fundamentals: concepts and approaches which will serve the
student through his entire practicing career. Speaking per-
sonally, I would have been helped much more in my overall
software engineering career by a course on how to apply
Hosier's lessons learned, or by a course on software economics,
than I have been by course material I had on optimal sorting
on a 2-tape machine with a poorly buffered memory, or on pre-
dicting the growth of truncation errors on machines with poorly designed arithmetic units. I'm not sure that today's
microprocessor courses on how to hack around the problems in
the Cromemco loader are much better from the standpoint of
teaching fundamentals. Thus, I think that a reasonable argument can be made that the software management and economics
topics above are appropriate for computer science departments.

This is borne out by Figure 1, which shows the estimated
half-life of various classes of techniques used by software
engineers. In the year 2000, today's students will find the
fundamental techniques of cost-benefit analysis and planning
and control still valuable and relevant, while the techniques
they learned in microprocessors and operating systems will be
largely out of date and unusable.

Good progress is being made by the IEEE/CS Subcommittee
on Software Engineering Education toward defining a Master's
curriculum in software engineering [Fairley (1979)]. However,

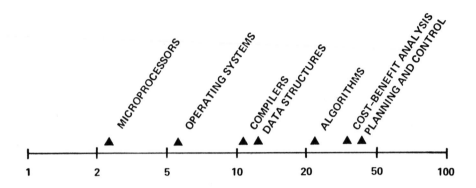

FIGURE 1. Half-life of software engineering techniques (years).

progress in implementing the curriculum is slow. At this writing, only one University (TCU, under A. J. Hoffman) has, to my knowledge, actually established a formal Master's degree in software engineering.

3. *Technology Transfer is Slow*

Over the past few years, I have been able to observe some of the ways in which software engineering technology is transferred into a large industrial organization such as TRW. The "technology transfer measuring stick" shown in Figure 2 is one attempt to characterize what it is that makes such an organization adopt a new technology item. If a paper is published which simply presents an idea which addresses a significant problem, the idea may be picked up and used, but rarely. (Sometimes we have done this, only to find that even the originator had subsequently discarded the idea, although not as pubicly as it was presented.) In general, software development people want to be assured that the idea has worked successfully in practice, on a job similar to theirs, and (ideally) by people who are available to apply it to their project.

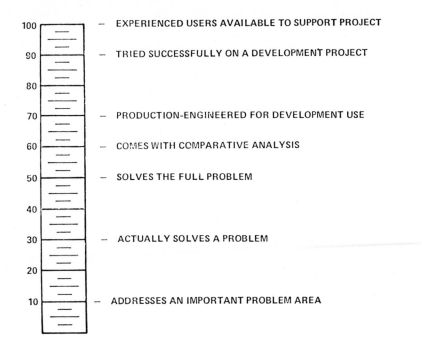

FIGURE 2.   Research Results: A Measuring Stick for Successful Technology Transfer.

This ideal is not always feasible, but in reviewing software engineering contributions which have been picked up most readily at TRW, they tend to cluster at the higher end of the measuring stick in Figure 2. Some examples are top-down structured programming [Baker (1975)], Pascal [Wirth (1971)], ISDOS [Teichroew-Hershey (1977)], PDL [Caine-Gordon (1975)], Concurrent Pascal [Brinch-Hansen (1977)], and Parnas' specification and design techniques [Parnas (1978, 1979); and Heninger, et al. (1978)].

I have found that the best way to judge whether a paper is at the higher or lower end of the technology transfer scale is to look at its Conclusions. If they say something like,

> "This technique has been implemented and found superior to other techniques for the following classes of problems: ..."

then the contribution will tend to be at the top of the scale.
If the Conclusions say something like,

> "Although this technique has not been
> implemented, the author believes ..."

or if the paper has no Conclusions at all, then the contribution will tend to be at the bottom of the scale. We can all
help to improve technology transfer by moving our contributions higher up the scale, even though it may mean publishing
fewer papers.

4. *We Resist the Required Discipline*

We are beginning to accept the fact that there is "A Discipline of Programming" [Dijkstra (1976)] which requires us
to accept constraints on our programming degrees of freedom
in order to achieve a more reliable and well-understood product. We are reaching the point where we are willing to tie
ourselves down more fully by declaring in advance our variable types, weakest preconditions, and the like. But our free
spirits still rebel at tieing ourselves down more fully by
declaring in advance just what software we are going to build,
how we are going to put it together, who is going to verify
it and how, and what is the user going to do with it once he
gets it. It's still much more attractive to jump in and start
laying code. I'm afraid that this particular problem will be
a long time in going away.

5. *We Have Our Role Models Mixed Up*

Another related factor inhibiting the progress of disciplined software engineering practice is something we call the
"Wyatt Earp Syndrome." The "Wyatt Earp" is the indispensible
programmer: the one who carries the critical program logic
and design decisions around in his head, never documenting
anything he does. When the inevitable crisis comes along,
only he can save the situation, coming on like Wyatt Earp
saving the town from the bad guys. All too often, the result
is that the indispensable programmer is given a raise or a

bonus, and becomes a hero or role model for other programmers in the organization. And in the process, the organization has become even more dependent on its Wyatt Earp than it was before.

The solution? Jerry Weinberg, a highly humanitarian person, has described it concisely: "If a programmer is indispensable, get rid of him as quickly as possible" [Weinberg (1971)].

6. We Often Take a Restricted View of Software Engineering

The engineering of large software systems is as complex as any engineering ventures in history. Even judging conservatively, a 1,000,000-instruction software product has at least 10,000 component functions (assuming 100 instructions per function), each of which can be specified and developed in at least two different ways. Thus, even at this function level, there are $2^{10,000}$, or about $10^{3,000}$, combinations of function choices which the software engineer must sort out.*

When dealing with this level of complexity, it is absolutely necessary to simplify things to make them intellectually tractable. In doing so, we often take a restricted view of "software engineering" which equates it to "programming methodology," and then proceed to tackle our programming problems.

Problems with the Restricted View

This restricted view is a good thing from the standpoint of clarifying our approach to programming tactics. However, software projects which have taken this restricted view exclusively, to the exclusion of the resource engineering and human relations aspects of software engineering, have unfortunately proceeded to relearn many of the lessons discussed above. One order-processing software project did a beautiful job of top-down, deductive structured programming, only to come to grief because it had not spent enough effort defining the

---

* One successful early software product JOSS [Shaw (1964)] was characterized as "10,000 small decisions, 99.9% of which were made correctly."

proper "top" of the system. As a result, the overall order-
processing system was more inefficient, error prone, and
frustrating to use than even its cumbersome manual predecessor. Another well-structured, modular, hierarchical real-time
system failed when it simply would not work in real time on
the user's workload - a fact that would have been evident by
an early workload characterization and resource analysis of
the system.

The need for using the broad rather than the restricted
view of software engineering is also seen in Figure 3, which
summarizes the problems in computer system acquisition found
in 151 U.S. General Accounting Office audits [GAO (1977)].
Although technology factors are a significant source of acquisition problems, it is clear from Figure 3 that the major
problem sources are more in the areas of acquisition planning
and project control.

Problems with the Sequential Approach

It would be convenient if we could perform a sequential
"separation of concerns" which neatly factored the software
engineering problem into a "programming-methodology" problem
and a separable set of problems which covered all other

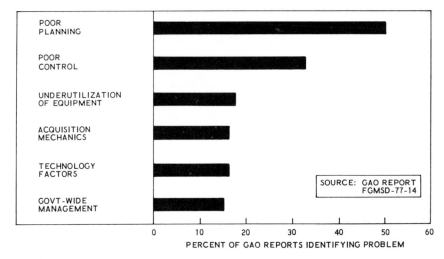

*FIGURE 3.   Problems with Computer System Acquisition and
Use in U.S. Government, 1965-1976*

considerations. There are two basic approaches for doing
this - the "deductive top-down" approach and the "tuning"
approach - but unfortunately they have not worked out well in
general practice.

In the "deductive top-down" approach, all of the resource-
engineering and human-relations problems are worked out in
advance. The result of this activity is a fully-defined requirements specification, which can then be frozen and used
as the basis of a deductive, top-down programming activity.
Unfortunately, this approach will not work in general because
of the fundamental volatility of software requirements. For
example, IBM's Santa Teresa software organization has found,
on a sample of roughly 1,000,000 instructions of software
produced per year to IBM-determined requirements, that the
average project experiences a 25% change in requirements during the period of its development [Climis (1979)].

The other approach is the "tuning" approach, in which the
software is developed deductively from a first-cut set of
requirements and then modified on the basis of user lessons
learned in the meantime. Unfortunately, this approach will
not work in general because of the inertia of user organizations. Once an initial software product is put into operation
(however inappropriate), users tend to develop operational
mechanisms to compensate for the deficiencies in the software;
these are extremely hard to change, once established. In
these cases, the degrees of freedom for tuning the system are
much more restricted than had been originally anticipated,
and a number of preferable modes of operation have become
practically foreclosed by organizational inertia.* In other
cases, such as in some medical information systems, the initial programming product was so far from being acceptable to
the doctors it was supposed to serve that the product was
scrapped entirely, leaving no opportunity for tuning at all.

---

* Here is a typical example: "You say you want to take
those redundancies out of the data base so we can simplify
our audit procedures? Well, that's nice, but it wouldn't
work. We've just finished negotiating agreements on our
audit procedures with Corporate Headquarters, and it would
take us a year or so to renegotiate."

The Broad View of Software Engineering

For these reasons, it is important not to restrict our
view of "software engineering" to cover only "programming
methodology," but to adopt a definition of "software engineering" which encompasses the *necessarily concurrent* concerns of
resource engineering and human relations. Fortunately, such
a definition is consistent with common dictionary [Webster
(1979)] definitions of "software" and "engineering."

> o *Software* is the entire set of programs,
>   procedures, and related documentation
>   associated with a system and especially
>   a computer system.
>
> o *Engineering* is the application of science
>   and mathematics by which the properties
>   of matter and the sources of energy in
>   nature are made useful to man in struc-
>   tures, machines, products, systems, and
>   processes.

Since the properties of matter and sources of energy over
which software has control are embodied in the capabilities
of computer equipment, we can combine the two definitions
above as follows:

> o *Software Engineering* is the application
>   of science and mathematics by which the
>   capabilities of computer equipment are
>   made useful to man via computer programs,
>   procedures, and associated documentation.

Discussion

This definition of "software engineering" contains two key
points which deserve further discussion. First, our definition of "software" includes a good deal more than just computer programs. Thus, learning to be a good software engineer means a good deal more than learning how to generate
computer programs. It also involves learning the skills required to produce good documentation, data bases, and operational procedures for computer systems.

The second key point is the phrase "useful to man." From
the standpoint of *practice*, this phrase places a responsibility upon us as software engineers to make sure that our software products are indeed useful to man. If we accept an
arbitrary set of specifications and turn them into a correct

computer program satisfying the specifications, we are not
discharging our full responsibility as software engineers.
We must also apply our skills and judgment to the job of
developing an appropriate set of specifications, and to the
job of ensuring that the resulting software does indeed make
the computer equipment perform functions that are useful to
man.   Thus, concerns for the social implications of computer
systems are part of the software engineer's job, and techniques for dealing with these concerns must be built into the
software engineer's practical methodology, rather than being
treated as a separate topic isolated from our day-to-day
practice.

From the standpoint of *learning*, the phrase "useful to
man" implies that the science and mathematics involved in
software engineering covers a good deal more than basic computer science.   For something to be useful to man, it must
satisfy a human need at a cost that man can afford.   Thus, the
science and mathematics we must learn to apply as software
engineers also includes the science of understanding human
needs and human relations, i.e., psychology; the science of
costs and values, i.e., economics; and the science of developing products within given cost budgets, i.e., management
science.

Software Engineering Curriculum Implications

From the standpoint of learning, therefore, I find the
current direction of evolution of the IEEE proposed master's
curriculum in Software Engineering [Fairley (1979)] somewhat
disappointing.   The first draft of the curriculum contained
both a course on Human Factors in Computing System Design and
a course on Security and Privacy.   In the second draft these
were reduced to a single course which somewhat awkwardly tries
to cover both topics together.   Neither draft is very strong
in the area of software engineering economics, although software management is appropriately highlighted in a course.
Again, given the dominance of these concerns in practical
software engineering situations, it is hoped that future iter-
ations of the IEEE curriculum recommendations will contain a

stronger emphasis on the broader view of software engineering.
(Author's Note: The third iteration is considerably stronger
in software economics, but still light on human factors.)

RECENT DEVELOPMENTS

This portion of the paper will convey some of the recent
developments in the field, as part of the "software engineering - as it is" charter of the paper.   For brevity and con-
venience, I will only cover developments since the "Software
Engineering" survey paper I wrote in 1976 [Boehm (1976)].   The
first section will cover recent developments in the "programming methodology" areas of
      1.   Requirements and Specifications
      2.   Program Design
      3.   Programming
      4.   Verification and Validation
      5.   Maintenance
The second section will cover recent developments in the more
broad-based areas of software engineering such as software
phenomenology and economics, software psychology, and human
factors in software engineering.

1.   Requirements and Specifications

There are three main approaches for expressing what a
software product is to do in a set of requirements specifications.   These are:
    1.   *Informal specifications.*   These are the traditional
        free-form natural-language specifications.   They re-
        quire virtually no training to write or read, but
        their ambiguity and lack of organization generally
        lead to serious problems with incompleteness, incon-
        sistency, and misunderstandings among the various
        groups of people (users, buyers, developers, testers,
        trainers, interfacers, etc.) who must use them to
        guide their software development activities.
    2.   *Formatted specifications.*   These are specifications
        expressed in a standardized syntax, which provides a
        framework for organizing the specifications and

performing basic consistency and completeness checks. They generally require a moderate level of training to read and write well, but can be mastered easily by average programmers. Their formatted nature precludes certain sources of ambiguity, but their imprecise semantics implies that other sources of error are still present (e.g., one can define and use a term such as "mode" or "mechanism" and not pin down precisely what it means).

3. *Formal specifications.* These are specifications expressed in a precise mathematical form, with both syntax and semantics rigorously defined. They require a good deal more expertise and training to be able to read and write, and a longer time to write than formatted specifications. However, they eliminate virtually all sources of imprecision and ambiguity in a specification, and provide a basis for constructing a correct program and mathematically verifying its equivalence to the specification.

A good deal of progress has been made in the last three years in the development and use of both formatted and formal specifications. In the area of formatted specifications, the two major automated goals ISDOS/CADSAT [Teichroew-Hershey (1977)] and SREM [Bell, et al. (1977); Alford (1977)] have continued to mature through use. ISDOS/CADSAT has added more powerful consistency and completeness checks, and a number of user-inspired improvements in data entry and output reports. SREM has become available on more host computers, has added capabilities to support business data processing and distributed processing applications, and has been used successfully by several organizations outside of its originators at TRW and the U.S. Army BMD Advanced Technology Center [Alford (1978)]. Nonautomated tools such as SADT [Ross-Schoman (1977)] have also experienced a significant expansion in the number and variety of successful users. In addition, other automated systems of formatted specification have been developed, such as AXES [Hamilton-Zeldin (1979)], a function-oriented specification method, and SAMM [Lamb, et al. (1978)], which appears

to be strongly based on SADT. A good review of formatted
specification techniques is found in [Ramamoorthy-So (1978)].

In the area of formal specifications, a good summary and
discussion of recent progress can be found in [Liskov-Berzins
(1979)] and in the discussion of this article by Parsons,
Goguen, Hamilton, and Zeldin in [Wegner (1979)]. Most significantly, formal specification techniques are beginning to
be used with success on nontrivial practice software products.
Examples are the use of SPECIAL [Roubine-Robinson (1977)] in
developing the (hopefully) secure operating systems PSOS
[Feiertag-Neumann (1979)] and KSOS [Berson-Barksdale (1979)],
and the use of AFFIRM [Musser (1979)] in the attempt to verify
the Delta military message-processing software [Gerhart-Wile
(1979)].

Also, some significant progress has been made at bridging
the gap between the more readable and easy-to-specify informal
and formatted specifications, and the more precise, unambigu-
ous formal specifications. One interesting approach is the
Specification Acquisition from Experts (SAFE) approach in
[Balzer, et al. (1977)], which provides automated tools to
help make an imprecise specification more precise. Another
highly significant achievement is the large (over 400 pages)
A-7 avionics software specification [Heninger, et al. (1978);
and Heninger (1979)]. This specification combines a great
deal of precision with a great deal of readability, and
handles the complexity of a large practical problem extremely
well.

The main result of all this progress is to expand the
domains in which formal and formatted specification techniques
are practical to use. The best way I have found to characterize these domains is shown in Figure 4. It shows that the
more expensive, time-consuming, expert-oriented formal methods
are most appropriate when the requirements are very stable and
don't need frequent rework (you can afford to use the formal
methods) and when the application requires a very high degree
of fault-freedom (you can't afford not to use the formal
methods). The increased power, efficiency, and practical
experience with formal and formatted specification techniques
is pushing their domains of applicability down (more and more)

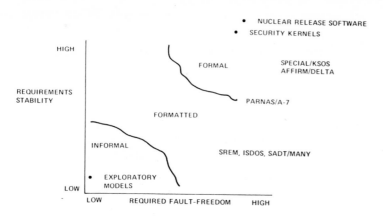

FIGURE 4. Specification methods - current domains of utility.

toward problems with less stable software requirements and lower requirements for fault-freedom, continually reducing the domain in which informal techniques are preferable.

2. Software Design

A good deal of progress has also been made in the area of software design. Considerable experience with earlier design techniques has been accumulated, with the general conclusions that the HIPO technique has been less successful; that Program Design Language (PDL) [Caine-Gordon (1975)] has been successful and demonstrably superior to flowcharts [Ramsey, et al. (1978)]; and that the various forms of structured or composite design [Yourdon (1975); Myers (1975), Yourdon-Constantine (1978), and DeMarco (1978)] have been highly successful.

Design techniques emphasizing data structuring have also been maturing, particularly those of [Jackson (1975)] and [Warnier (1974)]. The technology of life-cycle design took a significant step forward with the publication of Parnas' "Designing Software for East of Extension and Contraction" [Parnas (1978, 1979)], which provides sound guidelines for using information-hiding principles to organize software in

ways which make it easier to accommodate future changes.   A
good recent survey of software design techniques is [Freeman-
Wasserman (1977)].

A number of organizations are developing extremely ambitious, all-encompassing computer-aided-design systems for
software design, including capabilities for control structuring, data structuring, performance modeling, core budgeting,
complexity analysis, assertions, flow analysis, cost analysis,
and management tracking. These organizations would be well-
advised to proceed with caution: such systems can easily
collapse under their own weight. At least, this was our
experience with the DEVISE system [Boehm, et al. (1975)],
which included ISDOS and PDL as subsets, along with a number
of the abovementioned capabilities. Although the originators
were able to navigate reasonably well through the resulting
welter of data entry requirements and control options, most
other designers at TRW clearly preferred to use PDL. It was
easy to learn and use, and imposed fewer constraints on their
design approach. Our conclusion has been that a library of
simple, limited-purpose design aids is a preferable way to
proceed until we better understand the design process.

3. Programming

The most significant recent advance in programming methodology has been the constructive approach to developing correct programs or "programming calculus" formulated in
[Dijkstra (1975)], elaborated with numerous examples in
[Dijkstra (1976)], and discussed further in [Gries (1976)].
This approach provides a clean, powerful method for working
with a program specification to either derive a program structure which correctly implements the specification, or (just
as important) to identify portions of the specification which
are incomplete or inconsistent. At this point, it is becoming
clear that the approach does not fully address all the problems involved in the development of large-scale software and
user-oriented software (see the discussions by Gries, Horning,
Liskov, and Parnas in [Wegner (1979)] and the discussion of
"Problems with the Sequential Approach" above). However, the

concepts involved provide powerful tools for attacking many
of our most difficult programming problems.

A strong example of this power is given in the approach
of [Hoare (1978)] in applying the concepts of weakest preconditions, guarded commands, and indeterminacy to provide a
clear, disciplined set of techniques for dealing with the
extremely difficult area of cooperating sequential processes.
In the area of concurrent programming, a good deal of progress
has also been made in applying the Concurrent PASCAL language
to practical problems [Brinch-Hansen (1977, 1978); and
Stepczyk (1978)] and determining improvements to cover some
of the problems encountered with distributed monitors and with
efficiency. Good surveys of other work in distributed and
concurrent processing are given in [Stankovic-van Dam (1979)]
and [Bryant-Dennis (1979)].

In the area of programming languages, the most significant
development has been the progress toward the ADA language
sponsored by the U.S. Department of Defense [Fisher (1977);
and Ichbiah (1979)]. Although ADA has been widely criticized
for its wide scope, ambitious incorporation of new concepts,
and rapid timetable, it has come through so far as a well-
designed, responsive language with a very good chance of becoming the next-generation standard programming language for
a wide range of applications.

The amount of criticism directed toward ADA has been perhaps the most positive aspect of the entire ADA experience to
date. No other language has had anywhere near as much open
and broad-based review of its general and specific requirements and its preliminary and detailed design before proceeding into language development. In this respect, the ADA process provides a good model and base of experience for similar
developments of highly standardized software in the future.

4. *Verification and Validation*

Progress in formal program verification (proof of correctness) techniques was discussed, to some extent, in the remarks
above on formal specification techniques. Again, with respect
to Figure 4, the current progress in formal methods implies
that they already represent a viable option for application

to practical problems with very stable requirements and a very
high level of required fault freedom; and that their domain
of applicability in Figure 4 will continue to expand. A survey of current work in formal verification techniques is
given in [London (1979)].

Recent contributions have also given us a better understanding of what we should expect from formal verification
techniques - which is considerably less than a full guarantee
that the verified program is correct. A thorough analysis of
a number of errors in published program proofs has been given
in [Gerhart-Yelowitz (1976)]. An extensive discussion of
other difficulties with formal verification - understandability and credibility of proofs, scaling up to large systems,
program changes - and analogous experience in engineering and
mathematics has been provided in [De Millo, et al. (1979)],
with the general conclusion that the practical use of formal
techniques will never penetrate the lower regions of requirements stability and required fault-freedom in Figure 4.

Some progress has also been made on the theory of program
testing, based largely on the concepts in [Goodenough-Gerhart
(1975)]. Several papers by Hamlet, Richardson, and Ostrand
and Weyuker in the recent IEEE Workshop on Software Testing
and Test Documentation [Miller, et al. (1979)] explored further the concepts of test validity and test reliability, with
useful results in terms of improving test strategies. Some
new approaches with both theoretical and practical interest
have also been formulated: domain-testing [Cohen-White
(1977)] and program mutation [De Millo, et al. (1978)]. A
valuable discussion of these issues and techniques can be
found in [Goodenough (1979)] and the counterpoint discussions
of this article by Gerhart, Budd, et al., and White, et al.,
in [Wegner (1979)].

Considerable progress has been made in empirical studies
of program testing and verification. A number of highly useful studies by Howden have established at least some initial
results on the relative error-detection efficacy of various
testing and analysis methods [Howden (1977, 1978)]. When
these methods were tried on a common sample of programs containing 28 errors, they detected the following number of the

28 errors:

Path Testing - 18	Symbolic Execution - 17
Branch Testing - 6	Interface Analysis - 2
Structured Testing - 12	Anomaly Analysis - 4
Special Values - 17	Specification Requirements - 7

In the area of software reliability estimation, a valuable
study of the predictive performance of several techniques has
been performed by [Sukert (1978)]. This study showed that
the predictions were generally not very close to the actual
data, and were also highly sensitive to such features as the
sampling interval and the time of sampling initiation. This
behavior is most likely due to the failure of the independence
assumption underlying the prediction models, as the actual
error data was strongly conditioned by the sequence of test
objectives pursued during the various test phases. Some much
more successful predictions of software reliability have been
obtained in [Musa (1979)]. One strong contributing factor is
that the error data come from such contexts as trouble reports
on a steady-state time-sharing system, where the independence
assumption is more valid.

Finally, two extremely helpful books have been published
by Myers in the area of software testing and reliability
[Myers (1976, 1979)], containing a great deal of useful practical guidance in achieving reliable software.

5. *Software Maintenance*

Thanks to a recent survey [Lientz-Swanson (1978)] of 487
business data processing installations, we now have a clearer
picture of some of the gross characteristics of software maintenance. The survey confirmed that maintenance costs outweigh
development costs: the percentages of total software effort
break down as follows:

Development	:	43%
Maintenance	:	49%
Other	:	8%

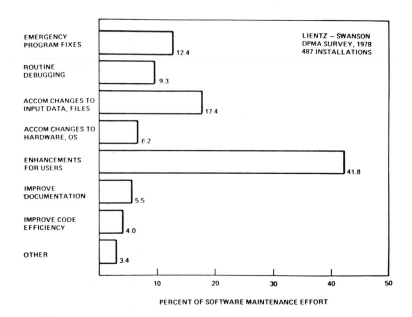

FIGURE 5. Distribution of software maintenance effort.

Figure 5 shows how the maintenance effort is typically distributed. The largest component is due to updates (41.8%), but significant percentages are due to software repair (21.7%), and accommodating changes to input data and files (17.4%). This last activity thus consumes almost 9% of the total software budget, which makes it a clear candidate for increased R&D to improve the process.

The most significant methodological advance to aid in designing for maintainability is the work on designing for extension and contraction in [Parnas (1978, 1979)]. Some useful maintainability design checklists and standards are given in [Lipow, et al. (1977)], and a good set of maintainability management guidelines is presented in [Munson (1978)]. Still, the software maintenance area is greatly underemphasized in current R&D efforts.

RECENT DEVELOPMENTS: INTEGRATED APPROACHES

This section of the paper discusses recent developments
in areas which integrate program engineering concerns with
other concerns such as human relations and software economics.

Software Psychology and Human Factors

The first major advance in software psychology was
Weinberg's excellent book *The Psychology of Computer Programming* [Weinberg (1971)]. Subsequent work [Weinberg (1972)]
established a significant correlation between components of
programmer performance and the objectives that programmers
are given to optimize. More recently, some very useful insights into programmer motivation were obtained in [Couger-
Zawacki (1978)], which showed that data processing personnel
are significantly different from other classes of workers in
the strength of their growth need and the weakness of their
social need. (One moral: promoting top programmers into
management is more likely to invoke the Peter Principle.)
Other similar insights are given in [Fitz-Enz (1978)].

More and more useful studies are being performed on corre-
lates of human performance in software situations, such as
the complexity-measure experiments in [Sheppard, et al.
(1979)], the database query experiments in [Schneiderman
(1978)], and the language experiments in [Gannon-Horning
(1975)]. Some very helpful studies and guidelines for engineering the software man-machine interface are discussed in
[Dzida, et al. (1978)] on interactive system design features,
in [Gilb-Weinberg (1977)] on humanized data entry via keyed
input, and in [Meister (1976)] on general man-machine task
structuring. A good bibliography of progress in the field is
[Atwood, et al. (1979)]. An even better general reference
will be the upcoming software psychology textbook
[Schneiderman (1979)].

Software Phenomenology and Economics

The general quantitative study of software phenomenology
has been the subject of two highly productive recent workshops [Lehman (1977); and Basili (1978)] covering such areas

as software cost modeling; measurement of software reliability, complexity, and other qualities; quantitative software psychology studies; software maintenance phenomena; and general problems of software data collection and analysis.

One trend observable from these workshops and related studies is a significant degree of progress in the area of software cost estimation. Some examples of cost estimation models with improved predictive capability based on their calibration to at least 20 project data points each are the Doty model [Herd, et al. (1977)]; the IBM-FSD model [Felix-Walston (1977)]; the Putnam model [Putnam (1978)]; the RCA PRICE S model [Freiman-Park (1979)]; and the TRW SCEP model [Boehm-Wolverton (1978)]. Each of these efforts has resulted not just in a model but also in an increased understanding of the major factors influencing software costs, and their distribution across the various software life-cycle phases and activities.

Two examples of the latter are shown in Figures 6 and 7, which summarize the results of an experiment recently conducted by the author, involving the development of the same small software product (an interactive software cost estimation model) by two 5-6 person teams.

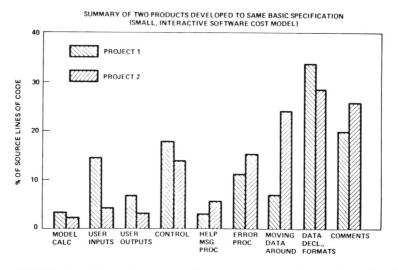

FIGURE 6. What does a software product do? Distribution of source code by function.

Figure 6 shows the distribution of the resulting lines of code by function. The results for the two products are quite similar; in particular, note that only 2-3% of the code actually implements the model: the other 97-98% is devoted to various user interface, error handling, declaration, and other housekeeping functions. Figure 7 shows the distribution of project effort by activity, based on timesheets filled out by the participants. The distribution tends to reinforce the thesis that software engineering involves a good deal more than programming, which consumed only 9-10% of the project's effort.

Other significant contributions in this area include the analysis of RADC's large software data base of over 300 projects [Nelson (1977)] to obtain strong correlations between software project effort and schedule and software product size in number of instructions; the software evolution dynamics studies summarized in [Belady-Lehman (1979)]; and the encyclopedic analysis of general data processing costs and economics in [Phister (1976)].

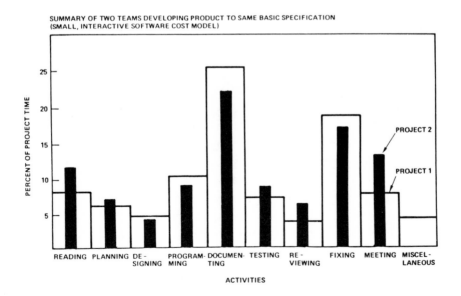

FIGURE 7. What does a software project do? Distribution of project time by activity.

CONCLUSIONS

In 1976, the software engineering field seemed to be pre-
occupied with what I called at the time *Area 1: detailed
design and coding of systems software by experts* in a relatively *economics-independent* context; while the most pressing
problems seemed to be in *Area 2: requirements analysis, design, test, and maintenance of applications software* by *tech-
nicians* in an *economics-driven* context. It is a real pleasure
to observe that in 1979 there is not only a good deal more
effort devoted to Area 2, but also that the effort is yielding
highly useful and solid results.

Other signs of the increased maturity and sophistication
of the field are the more careful qualifications and distinctions made in presenting and analyzing software engineering
techniques today. A few years ago, the field seemed to abound
with simplistic panaceas such as:

- o "Proof techniques will guarantee reliable
  software."
- o "Put the processing on a chip and the software problem will go away."
- o "More detailed standards and procedures will
  make everybody good software managers."
- o "Automatic programming is just around the
  corner, and programmers will all be out of
  jobs."
- o "Eliminating GOTO's will reduce your software budget by 50%."

Nowadays, these oversimplified statements are heard very
rarely, and there is much more emphasis on establishing the
particular problem domains in which a given technique is
effective or preferable to others. This has forced us to
accept the fact that the software field is not a simple one,
and that if anything, it is getting more complex at a faster
rate than we can put it in order. But I suspect that most of
us would agree with Bill Wulf's assessment of this trend
[Wulf (1979)]:

> "The research trends described here will
> undoubtedly improve the situation, but his-
> tory suggests that our aspirations will grow
> at least as fast as the technology to satisfy
> them. I, for one, would not want it any
> other way."

REFERENCES

Alford, M. W. (Jan. 1977). A requirements engineering methodology for real-time processing requirements, *IEEE Trans.
Software Engr.*, 60-68.

Alford, M. W. (Nov. 1978). Software Requirements Engineering
Methodology (SREM) at the age of two, *Proceeding, COMPAC
78*, IEEE, 332-339.

Atwood, M. E., *et al.* (Jun. 1979). "Annotated Bibliography
on Human Factors in Software Development," U.S. Army ARI
Technical Report P-79-1.

Baker, F. T. (Jun. 1975). Structured programming in a production programming environment, *IEEE Trans. Software Engr.*,
241-253.

Balzer, R., Goldman, N., and Wile, D. (Jun. 1977). The infer-
ence of domain structure from informal process descriptions, *ACM SIGART Newsletter.*

Basili, V. R. (ed.) (Aug. 1978). "Proceedings, Second Software Life-Cycle Management Workshop," IEEE Catalog No.
78CH 1390-4C.

Belady, L. A., and Lehman, M. M. (1979). Characteristics of
large systems, *In:* P. Wegner (ed.), "Research Directions
in Software Technology," MIT Press, Cambridge, MA.

Bell, T. E., Bixler, D. C., and Dyer, M. E. (Jan. 1977). An
extendable approach to computer-aided software requirements engineering, *IEEE Trans. Software Engr.*, 49-59.

Berson, T. A., and Barksdale, Jr., G. L. (1979). KSOS-devel-
opment methodology for a secure operating system, *Proceedings, 1979 NCC*, 365-371.

Boehm, B. W. (Dec. 1976). Software engineering, *IEEE Trans.
Computers*, 1226-1241.

Boehm, B. W., and Wolverton, R. W. (1978). Software cost
modeling: some lessons learned, *In:* V. R. Basili (ed.),
"Proceedings, Second Software Life-Cycle Management Workshop," IEEE Catalog No. 78CH 1390-4C.

Boehm, B. W., McClean, R. L., and Urfrig, D. B. (Mar. 1975).
Some experience with automated aids to the design of
large scale reliable software, *IEEE Trans. Software Engr.*,
125-133.

Brinch Hansen, P. (1977). "The Architecture of Concurrent
    Programs," Prentice-Hall, Inc., Englewood Cliffs, NJ.
Brinch Hansen, P. (May 1978). Network: A multiprocessor
    program, *IEEE Trans. Software Engr.*, 194-198.
Bryant, R. E., and Dennis, J. B. (1979). Concurrent program-
    ming, *In:* P. Wegner (ed.), "Research Directions in Soft-
    ware Technology," MIT Press.
Caine, S. H., and Gordon, E. K. (1975). PDL: A tool for
    software design, *Proceedings, 1975 NCC*, 271-276.
Climis, T. (Feb. 1979). Software cost estimation, presenta-
    tion at NSIA Software Workshop, Buena Park, CA.
Cohen, E. I., and White, L. J. (Aug. 1977). "A Finite Domain-
    Testing Strategy for Computer Program Testing," Ohio State
    Univ., TR-77-13.
Couger, J. D., and Zawacki, R. A. (Sep. 1978). What motivates
    DP professionals?, *Datamation*, 116-123.
DeMarco, T. (1978). "Structured Analysis and System Specifi-
    cation," Yourdon Press, New York.
DeMillo, R. A., Lipton, R. J., and Sayward, F. E. (Apr. 1978).
    Hints on test data selection: Help for the practicing
    programmer, *Computer*, 34-41.
DeMillo, R. A., Lipton, R. J., and Perlis, A. J. (May 1979).
    Social processes and proofs of theorems and programs,
    Comm. ACM, 271-280.
Dijkstra, E. W. (Aug. 1975). Guarded commands, nondeterminacy
    and formal derivation of programs, *Comm. ACM*.
Dijkstra, E. W. (1976). "A Discipline of Programming,"
    Prentice-Hall, Inc., Englewood Cliffs, NJ.
Dzida, W., Herda, S., and Itzfeldt, W. D. (Jul. 1978). User-
    perceived quality of interactive systems, *IEEE Trans.
    Software Engr.*, 270-275.
Fairley, R. E. (Feb. 1979). "MSE-79: A Recommended Masters
    Curriculum in Software Engineering," Colorado State Univ.
Feiertag, R. J., and Neumann, P. G. (1979). The foundations
    of a Probably Secure Operating System (PSOS), *Proceedings,
    1979 NCC*, 329-334.
Felix, C. P., and Walston, C. E. (1977). A method of program-
    ming measurement and estimation, *IBM Sys. J., 16(1)*.

Fisher, D. A. (Oct. 1977). The common programming language of the Department of Defense, *Proceedings, AIAA/NASA/IEEE/ACM Computers in Aerospace Conference*, 297-307.

Fitz-Enz, J. (Sep. 1978). Who is the DP professional?, *Datamation*, 124-129.

Freeman, P., and Wasserman, A. I. (1977). "Tutorial on Software Design Techniques" (2nd ed.), IEEE Catalog No. 76CH 1145-2-C.

Freiman, F. R., and Park, R. E. (Feb. 1979). "The PRICE Software Cost Model," RCA Price Systems, Cherry Hill, NJ.

Gannon, J. D., and Horning, J. J. (Jun. 1975). Language design for programming reliability, *IEEE Trans. Software Engr.*, 179-191.

U.S. General Accounting Office (Mar. 1977). "Problems Found with Government Acquisition and Use of Computers from November 1965 to December 1976," GAO, Washington, DC, Report FGMSD-77-14.

Gerhart, S. L., and Yelowitz, L. (Sep. 1976). Observations of Fallibility in Applications of Modern Programming Methodologies, *IEEE Trans. Software Engr.*, 195-207.

Gerhart, S. L., and Wile, D. S. (Mar. 1979). Preliminary report on the delta experiment: Specification and verification of a multiple user file updating module, *Proceedings, Specifications of Reliable Software Conference*, IEEE, 198-211.

Gilb, T., and Weinberg, G. M. (1977). "Humanized Input," Winthrop, Inc., Cambridge, MA.

Goodenough, J. B. (1979). A survey of program testing issues, *In:* P. Wegner (ed.), "Research Directions in Software Technology," MIT Press.

Goodenough, J. B., and Gerhart, S. L. (Jun. 1975). Toward a theory of test data selection, *IEEE Trans. Software Engr.*, 156-173.

Gries, D. (Dec. 1976). An illustration of current ideas on the derivation of correctness proofs and correct programs, *IEEE Trans. Software Engr.*, 238-243.

Hamilton, M., and Zeldin, S. (1979). The relationship of design and verification, *Journal of Systems and Software*, 1(1).

Heninger, K. (Mar. 1979). Specifying software requirements for complex systems: New techniques and their application, *Proceedings, Specifications of Reliable Software Conference*, IEEE, 1-14.

Heninger, K., Kallander, J., Parnas, D. L., and Shore, J. (Nov. 1978). "Software Requirements for the A-7E Aircraft," Naval Research Laboratory Report 3876.

Herd, J. R., *et al.* (Jun. 1977). "Software Cost Estimation Study - Study Results," RADC-TR-77-220, Vol. 1.

Hoare, C. A. R. (Aug. 1978). Communicating sequential processes, *Comm. ACM*, 666-677.

Hosier, W. A. (Jun. 1961). Pitfalls and safeguards in real-time digital systems with emphasis on programming, *IRE Transactions on Engineering Management*, 99-115.

Howden, W. E. (1977). "Symbolic Testing - Design Techniques, Costs, and Effectiveness," NBS Report GR 77-89, NTIS No. PB268517.

Howden, W. E. (Jul. 1978). Theoretical and empirical studies of program testing, *IEEE Trans. Software Engr.*, 293-298.

Ichbiah, J. D., *et al.* (Jun. 1979). Rationale for the design of the ADA programming language, and Preliminary ADA reference manual, *ACM SIGPLAN Notices*.

Jackson, M. A. (1975). "Principles of Program Design," Academic Press.

Lamb, S. S., Lack, V. G., Peters, L. J., and Smith, G. L. (Nov. 1978). SAMM: A modeling tool for requirements and design specification, *Proceedings, COMPSAC 78*, IEEE, 48-53.

Lehman, M. M. (ed.). (Aug. 1977). "Software Phenomenology. Proceedings, U.S. Army Software Life Cycle Management Workshop."

Lientz, B. P., and Swanson, E. B. (Apr. 1979). Software maintenance: A user/management tug-of-war, *Data Management*, 26-30.

Lipow, M., White, B. B., and Boehm, B. W. (Nov. 1977). "Software Quality Assurance: An Acquisition Guidebook," TRW-SS-77-07.

Liskov, B. H., and Berzins, V. (1979). An appraisal of pro-
    gram specifications, *In:* P. Wegner (ed.), "Research
    Directions in Software Technology," MIT Press, Cambridge,
    MA.

London, R. L. (1979). Program verification, *In:* P. Wegner
    (ed.), "Research Directions in Software Technology, MIT
    Press, Cambridge, MA.

Magers, C. S. (Jun. 1978). Managing software development
    in microprocessor projects, *Computer*, 34-42.

Meister, D. (1976). "Behavioral Foundations of System Devel-
    opment," John Wiley & Sons, Inc., New York.

Miller, E., *et al*. (Mar. 1979). Workshop Report: Software
    testing and test documentation, *Computer*, 98-107.

Munson, J. B. (Nov. 1978). Software maintainability: A
    practical concern for life-cycle costs, *Proceedings,
    COMPSAC 78*, 54-59.

Musa, J. D. (1979). Software reliability measures applied to
    system engineering, *Proceedings, 1979 NCC*, 941-946.

Musser, D. R. (Mar. 1979). Abstract data type specifications
    in the affirm system, *Proceedings, Specifications of
    Reliable Software Conference*, IEEE, 47-57.

Myers, G. J. (1975). "Reliable Software Through Composite
    Design," Petrocelli-Chanter.

Myers, G. J. (1976). "Software Reliability," John Wiley &
    Sons, Inc., New York.

Myers, G. J. (1979). "The Art of Software Testing," John
    Wiley & Sons, Inc., New York.

Nelson, R. (1977). "Software Data Collection and Analysis at
    RADC," Rome, NY.

Parnas, D. L. (1978-1979). Designing software for ease of
    extension and contraction, *Proceedings, ICSE3*, May 1978,
    pp. 264-277; and *IEEE Trans. Software Engr.*, Mar. 1979,
    128-137.

Phister, Jr., M. (1976). "Data Processing Technology and
    Economics," Santa Monica Publishing Co., Santa Monica, CA.

Putnam, L. H. (Jul. 1978). A general empirical solution to
    the macro software sizing and estimating problem, *IEEE
    Trans. Software Engr.*, 345-361.

Ramamoorthy, C. V., and So, H. H. (1978). Software require-
    ments and specifications: Status and perspectives, *In:*
    C. V. Ramamoorthy and R. T. Yeh, "Tutorial: Software
    Methodology," IEEE Catalog No. EHO 142-0, 43-164.

Ramsey, H. R., Atwood, M. E., and Van Doren, J. R. (Sep. 1978).
    "A Comparative Study of Flowcharts and Program Design
    Languages for the Detailed Procedural Specification of
    Computer Programs," U.S. Army ARI Technical Report TR-78-
    A22.

Rauscher, T. G. (Jun. 1978). A unified approach to microcom-
    puter software development, *Computer*, 44-54.

Ross, D. T., and Schoman, Jr., K. E. (Jan. 1977). Structured
    analysis for requirements definition, *IEEE Trans. Soft-
    ware Engr.*, 6-15.

Roubine, O., and Robinson, L. (Jan. 1977). "SPECIAL Reference
    Manual," SRI International, Menlo Park, CA.

Shaw, J. C., (1964). JOSS: A designer's view of an experi-
    mental on-line computing system, *Proceedings, 1964 FJCC,*
    455-464.

Sheppard, S. B., Curtis, B., Milliman, P., Borst, M. A., and
    Love, T. (1979). First-year results from a research pro-
    gram on human factors in software engineering, *Proceed-
    ings, 1979 NCC*, 1021-1028.

Shneiderman, B. (Dec. 1978). Improving the human factors
    aspect of database interactions, *ACM Trans. Database
    Systems*, 417-439.

Shneiderman, B. (1979). "Software Psychology," Prentice-Hall,
    Inc., Englewood Cliffs, NJ.

Stankovic, J. A., and van Dam, A. (1979). Research directions
    in (cooperative) distributed processing, *In:* P. Wegner
    (ed.), "Research Directions in Software Technology, MIT
    Press, Cambridge, MA.

Stepczyk, F. (Nov. 1978). A case study in real-time distrib-
    uted processing design, *Proceedings, COMPSAC 78*, 514-519.

Sukert, A. N. (Nov. 1978). A four-project empirical study of
    software error prediction models, *Proceedings, COMPSAC 78*,
    577-582.

Teichroew, D., and Hershey, III, E. A. (Jan. 1977). PSL/PSA: A computer-aided technique for structured documentation and analysis of information processing systems, *IEEE Trans. Software Engr.*, 41-48.

Thayer, R. H., Pyster, A., and Wood, R. C. (May 1979). "Major Issues in Software Engineering Project Management," Sacramento Air Logistics Center.

Warnier, J. D. (1974). "Logical Construction of Programs," Van Nostrand Reinhold, New York.

"Webster's New Collegiate Dictionary," (1979). G&C Merriam Co.

Wegner, P. (ed.) (1979). "Research Directions in Software Technology," MIT Press, Cambridge, MA.

Weinberg, G. M. (1971). "The Psychology of Computer Programming," Van Nostrand Reinhold, New York.

Weinberg, G. M. (Nov. 1972). The psychology of improved programming performance, *Datamation*.

Wirth, N. (1971). The programming language pascal, *Acta Informatica*, 35-63.

Wulf, W. A. (1979). Comments on current practice, *In:* P. Wegner (ed.), "Research Directions in Software Technology," MIT Press, Cambridge, MA.

Yourdon, E. (1975). "Techniques of Program Structure and Design," Prentice-Hall.

Yourdon, E., and Constantine, L. L. (1978). "Structured Design," (2nd ed.), Yourdon Press, New York.

SOFTWARE ADAPTABILITY

AND

PROGRAM TRANSFORMATION[1]

Dr. *James M. Boyle*

Applied Mathematics Division
Argonne National Laboratory
Argonne, Illinois

WHAT IS THE ROLE OF ADAPTABILITY IN SOFTWARE ENGINEERING?

Software engineering is the art, science, and discipline
of producing reliable software efficiently. It is thus fundamentally concerned (as are other engineering disciplines)
with improving the economics of production. The role of research on software adaptability and automatic software adaptation in software engineering arises from its promise in
addressing this economic concern.

There are at least three general strategies for improving
the economics of endeavors in which a single component, such
as software, constitutes a major portion of the cost. The
most obvious is to reduce the cost of the expensive component.
Indeed, much software engineering research has been devoted
to developing disciplines and tools which do just that. In
general, these disciplines involve committing more resources
to the design and production of software in order to produce
programs that are reliable initially, so that fewer resources
need be expended on testing and correcting faulty programs.
Carrying out a proof of correctness represents an extreme
form of such techniques, for essentially all resources are
committed to the proof, which then guarantees that the

---

[1]*Work performed under the auspices of the U.S. Department
of Energy.*

program meets its specifications without need of testing.
These programming disciplines make software much more reliable, but it seems unlikely that they will actually make it
cheap to produce, for the design and implementation phases
remain labor-intensive.

A second general strategy is to reduce the need for the
costly component. It is applicable in some areas of software
engineering, for example when the willingness to let rela-
tively-cheap hardware stand idle permits one to do without
relatively-expensive multiprogramming operating system software [see Tsichritzis (1980)]. Opportunities to apply this
strategy are limited, however, for it cannot eliminate the
software (or its equivalent) which defines a particular
application.

A third general strategy, which becomes especially important when costs have already been reduced as far as practic-
able, is to make maximal use of the high-cost component. This
strategy is being increasingly applied in various industries
where not one, but a whole family, of aircraft, computers,
etc., are built using the same basic design and the same production techniques. Such an approach does nothing to reduce
the cost of a design -- in fact, it may even increase it
slightly -- but it does permit that cost to be amortized over
several products instead of just one, thereby improving the
overall economy of production. Moreover, customers are likely
to be pleased to have a selection of products tailored and
optimized to various situations rather than having to accept
a single compromise product.

*Should not, then, software be produced in the same way, so
that each program written is regarded as the progenitor of a
whole family, each member of which is adapted to some particular circumstance?*

Of course, it should, and one might argue that certain
kinds of software (notably operating systems) have been produced in this way. However, the adaptability of most operating system software is obtained by means of options (e.g.,
"sysgen options") which select different segments of code or
selectively eliminate segments of code. Because these segments can combine in an immense number of ways as different

combinations of options are chosen, this approach to adaptability aggravates the reliability problem instead of contributing to its solution.

The key to effectively applying the strategy of making
maximal use of a costly resource is to recognize that *it is
software reliability, not software, that is expensive to produce.*

Thus the kind of software adaptation of primary interest
is that in which new programs are derived in ways which *preserve* the dearly-bought reliability of the programs being
adapted. By means of such reliability-preserving adaptations,
true economies in the production of software can be achieved.

Introducing the notion of reliability-preserving adaptations raises a number of questions: What qualities of a program make it easy to adapt? What characterizes the range of
programs that can be obtained as adaptations of a given one?
What guarantees the preservation of reliability? How can
adapted programs be made efficient? How can adaptation be
automated? I believe these will be significant software
engineering research questions for the next five to ten years;
nonetheless, the outlines of answers to some of them have become clear enough to discuss in the following sections. First,
however, I wish to give a concrete example of a use of software adaptation of the type being discussed.

AN APPLICATION OF RELIABLE ADAPTATION

Techniques of reliability-preserving automated program
adaptation have been applied in a rudimentary way in the development of LINPACK, a package of FORTRAN subroutines for
the solution of systems of linear equations [Dongarra, Bunch,
Moler, and Stewart (1979)]. Even though the adaptations performed were relatively modest, a four-fold reduction in the
number of subroutines to be written by hand, as well as an
increase in uniformity and reliability, was achieved for the
initial version of LINPACK, and further improvements in this
ratio are possible.

The use of adaptation in LINPACK arose from the following
observations: (1) subroutines to solve linear systems whose

coefficients are real, complex, real double-precision, or
complex double-precision numbers were required; (2) the algorithms are the same regardless of the data-type; and (3) the
programs for complex data contain sufficient information to
serve as a prototype permitting the derivation of the programs for the other three types. The latter is the key insight, for both xxy and $xxconjugate(y)$ in the complex version
map to xxy in the real version, making it impossible to invert
the process and take the real version as the prototype.
(LINPACK contains no full-precision constants; extension from
single to double precision is not a problem.)

The adaptations were automated by writing sets of program transformations for the TAMPR system [see Boyle (1977)]
which describe in general the processes for converting a program for complex data to one for real data (assuming the
latter computation can be done entirely in the real domain)
and for converting a program for single-precision data to one
for double-precision data. These two sets of transformations
can be considered to be functions, called *realization functions*, whose domains and ranges are programs [see Boyle
(1977)]. Calling the first R and the second D, and letting
a complex prototype program be represented by p, the LINPACK
realizations required in (1) were obtained as:

$$R(p), \ p, \ D(R(p)), \text{ and } D(p)$$

In addition to these realizations prepared by TAMPR for
the first release of LINPACK, others are under consideration
for future release. One of these is a programmed-complex
double-precision version, which would be useful on 32-bit
computers whose FORTRAN compilers do not support double-precision complex arithmetic. In this version, each complex
variable or array is represented by a pair of double-precision variables or arrays containing, respectively, its real
and imaginary parts, and complex computations are expanded
according to their definitions in terms of operations on real
and imaginary parts. A preliminary set of transformations
implementing a complex to programmed-complex realization function PC was done by S. J. Hague of the NAG Library Central
Office (1978). His work on this problem was especially interesting because the use of transformations made it easy for

him to apply his knowledge of numerical analysis to the problem of "generating code" for complex operations. This is a rather subtle problem, especially for division and absolute value when floating-point overflow and underflow can occur, and one which is frequently not treated correctly by compilers. With this realization function the required LINPACK version could be obtained as: $D(PC(p))$; the single-precision version $PC(p)$ could also be produced if desired.

A second realization being considered is a very high efficiency one. The routines in the initial version of LINPACK are fairly efficient, but in some places efficiency was compromised in order to maintain the readability, and hence the pedagogical value, of the programs. One of these compromises is that the LINPACK programs are written using the Basic Linear Algebra subprograms (BLAs) of Lawson, Hanson, Kincaid and Krogh (1980) in order to provide a high-level representation of the algorithms. On many computers, faster execution results if these routines (which compute such things as dot products, index of the maximum element of a vector, etc.) are replaced by in-line code. A set of transformations for this realization function $(\not{B})$ has been written and is described by Boyle and Matz (1977). Once BLA calls have been eliminated, further improvements in efficiency can be obtained by unrolling loops (UL), see Dongarra and Hinds (1979), and Loveman (1977). Finally, for some machines with naive FORTRAN compilers, more efficient code will be produced if two-dimensional arrays are replaced by one-dimensional ones; transformations for such a realization function (OD) could probably be written, although the existing LINPACK prototypes are not ideal for applying it. Because it is inefficient to apply complicated realization functions many times, the very high efficiency version of LINPACK will probably be produced by first deriving:

$$UL(\not{B}(OD(p)))$$

and then constructing needed realizations from it using R, D, and PC.

From an engineering and economic point of view, three things stand out in regard to software adaptability in LINPACK: (1) From each prototype program twelve useful versions can be

produced automatically. (2) Even though the transformations
implementing the realization functions have not been formally
proven correct, they have been tested; furthermore, they are
expressed at a high enough level that they can be "seen" to
be correct. Thus each of the twelve realizations inherits
the reliability of its prototype and hence requires only mini-
mal testing. (3) Because the realization functions are
fairly general, they can (as illustrated) be freely composed,
thus multiplying their cost-effectiveness.

From a software engineering research point of view, the
experience using automatic program adaptation in LINPACK,
together with some of the results of other investigators,
notably Bauer (1976) and Burstall and Darlington (1977),
enables one to sketch the answers to some of the research
questions posed at the end of the previous section. To understand what makes software adaptation easy, it helps to ask:

WHAT MAKES SOFTWARE ADAPTATION DIFFICULT?

The systematic adaptations used in LINPACK may be con-
trasted with a much more typical, and, unfortunately, nearly
worst-case, adaptation: adapting a moderately large applications program, written for a particular computer with no
thought of transportability, to work on a computer of different architecture. The basic problem is the same in both
cases, namely to produce a program which performs essentially
the same computation as the original but is tuned to a different environment. But the point of departure differs radically,
for the prototype in this latter instance corresponds most
closely to the real, one-dimensional, unrolled, BLA-less
version of a LINPACK program.

The difficulties in performing such an adaptation can be
seen clearly by considering an analogy from aeronautics. Suppose one has a design for a supersonic, carrier-based fighter
aircraft, such as that illustrated in Figure 1. The worst-
case program adaptation problem can be likened to being asked
to convert this design into one meeting the specifications
for a commercial passenger jumbo-jet such as, say, the A300-
Airbus shown in Figure 2.

FIGURE 1. Representation of a supersonic, carrier-based, fighter aircraft.

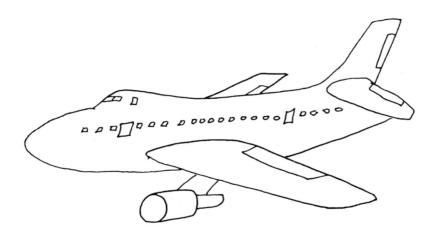

FIGURE 2. Representation of the specifications for a commerical passenger jumbo-jet aircraft.

Of course, the analogy is not complete, for the people who work with aircraft designs are normally knowledgable about airplanes, whereas in computing the same person may be asked to convert a reactor simulation program one month and a statistical package the next, and he is unlikely to be an expert in either field. I assume, therefore, that anyone mad enough

to request the conversion of the design for a fighter into
one for a passenger airplane would have it done by someone
who knew nothing about airplanes.

It can readily be understood, then, that *the central difficulty in performing the adaptation* under these circumstances
lies in recovering the abstract concept of airplane from the
fighter design. In the first place, it will be difficult to
infer whether a given aspect of the fighter design is an
aspect of all aircraft, and thus must be reflected in the design for the Airbus, or whether it is simply an aspect of the
adaptation to the specifications for the fighter. Secondly,
the fighter design is highly optimized to its task, and,
therefore, some aspects of the concept of airplane which are
irrelevant for that task may have been removed entirely from
the fighter design and therefore may not be recoverable at
all.

I assume that the person performing the conversion does
the best he can in the face of these difficulties, producing
a design corresponding to the illustration in Figure 3.

FIGURE 3. Representation of the results of adapting the
design of Figure 1 to the specifications of Figure 2.

Some of its more bizarre features can be explained as follows:
the adaptor was unable to satisfy himself that such features
as the machine guns and rockets were not part of the concept
of airplane, so, being a cautious fellow, he left them in the
design. About the arresting hook he was more confident, reasoning that the hook is like a kite-tail, and since a tail is
vital to a kite's stability, the same must be true for aircraft. Finally, the specifications for the Airbus called for
the inclusion of galleys, but he was not able to show that
they would not destroy airworthiness, so he had to leave them
out. This omission resulted in a number of dissatisfied customers!

It is no wonder that the typical program adaptation is
expensive, less than satisfactory, and would be virtually
impossible to automate. These observations also suggest that
there is more justification than usually admitted for the oft-
heard statement that one would rather write his own program
from scratch than adapt an existing one written for a different computer architecture.

WHAT MAKES ADAPTATION EASY?

If one actually wished to design an Airbus, he would not,
of course, start from the design for a specific fighter plane,
but rather from the abstract concept of "airplane-in-general",
or from increasingly more concrete (but still abstract) intermediate concepts like "jet aircraft", "subsonic jet aircraft",
"subsonic jet passenger aircraft", or "subsonic jumbo-jet passenger aircraft". Nothing in these concepts needs to be discarded in order to produce a design meeting the specification
of Figure 2; only additional decisions -- how many passengers,
how many engines, what range -- need to be made.

So, too, should a program adaptation begin from an
abstract version of the program -- one which has not yet been
tailored and optimized to a particular computer, to a particular data representation, and to a particular subproblem. In
this way, the effort of the adaptation is entirely concentrated on achieving its goals, and not wasted attempting to separate the essential and non-essential aspects of the behavior

of the program. In retrospect one can see that this was indeed a feature of the LINPACK adaptations, for the programs
describing the solution of linear systems for complex data in
terms of BLA calls and two-dimensional arrays are the most
general (and hence most abstract) of the realizations discussed. From these prototypes the other realizations are
obtained as answers to questions of the form: "How can the
execution of the prototype be *simplified* if I assume x?" where
x is "the data are real" or "in-line code is faster than sub-
program calls" or "loop overhead is non-negligible", etc.

Abstraction is clearly a key feature in successful adaptation of both programs and aircraft. However, from the aircraft analogy, one might conclude that program adaptation were
too complicated to automate, for even starting from a relatively low-level abstraction such as subsonic jumbo-jet passenger aircraft, a tremendous amount of engineering work (and
art) is required to produce a design for the Airbus. Thus one
may ask, with respect to automation:

DOES ABSTRACTION MAKE PROGRAM ADAPTATION EASY ENOUGH?

I believe that it does. The reason that automatic adaptation is possible for software but not for aircraft designs is
that *programs are mathematical objects that can be manipulated
according to algebraic rules.* One of the best discussions of
this idea is to be found in the recent Turing Lecture by
Backus (1978); it is also discussed by Arsac (1979) and
Burstall and Darlington (1977). This mathematical aspect of
programs means that it should be possible to formalize and
automate their manipulation (with much the same problems and
prospects as symbolic algebraic manipulation).

Abstract programs are especially rich in this mathematical
aspect. First of all, they are written at a higher level than
most programs and hence are closer to the formal mathematical
theory on which the *algorithm* they implement is based. (To
take an example from mathematical software: abstract linear
algebra programs may be written in terms of matrices and matrix operations instead of in terms of loops, indices, sub-
scripted variables, and scalar operations.) Secondly, the

behavior of the abstract data and operations can often be
described axiomatically [see, among many others, Partsch and
Broy (1979)]. Such an axiomatic characterization provides
two major benefits: it is fundamental to proving the correctness of the abstract program; and it describes (exactly) the
properties of the abstract data and operations which must be
preserved in making a concrete adaptation of the abstract
program.

There is thus a very strong analogy (perhaps, even iden-
tity) between constructing a concrete realization of an abstract program and making a concrete interpretation of an
abstract mathematical theory. For example, in studying a new
mathematical entity, one may realize that certain of its properties are reminiscent of theorems of group theory. If he
then verifies that the new entity and one of its operations
satisfy the axioms of group theory, all of the theorems of
group theory can be reinterpreted for the new entity, and are
known to be true for it without proof. In almost exactly the
same way, if one has an abstract program and has devised a
possible concrete implementation for its axiomatically characterized abstract data and operations, *he need only verify that
the implementation satisfies these axioms in order to know
that all properties provable about the abstract program (including, perhaps, its correctness and termination) will be
true of a concrete adaptation constructed using that implementation.* Reliability-preserving adaptation, indeed!

The process of adapting an abstract program thus consists
of adding information to it (i.e., making decisions) indicating how abstractions are to be represented more concretely.
In this process, the properties of the abstract program are
preserved, but they are, of course, augmented by additional
ones which were not true of the abstract program, just as, for
example, the integers have many properties besides those
implied by the fact that they form a group under addition.
Thus when undergoing adaptation, a program passes through a
hierarchy of abstractions, each of which is more concrete than
its predecessor, in the sense that it is more tuned to the
final environment and capable of giving rise to a smaller
number of differing adaptations.

These observations show in detail why a concrete program
is an unsatisfactory starting point for an adaptation: namely,
it *has properties which are irrelevant to meeting its speci-*
fications.   In the LINPACK example discussed above, if one
were to examine the realization employing one-dimensional
arrays in detail, he might observe that it has the property
that elements of the coefficient matrix of the order-n linear
system which are adjacent in a row (e.g., $A_{i,j}$ and $A_{i,j+1}$)
are separated by exactly n locations in the one-dimensional
array representing the matrix.   If now he wishes to adapt the
program (say to use a two-dimensional array or to use secondary storage), he must answer such questions as: is this very-
specific property strictly necessary to the correct functioning of the program?   If not, is some related consistency
property (e.g., regular spacing m locations apart, $m \geq n$)
necessary?   Or is this apparent property utterly accidental
and not at all related to the correct functioning of the program?   To answer these questions by looking only at the concrete program can be extremely difficult.   On the other hand,
if one examines a corresponding abstract program formulated
in terms of matrix data and operations (a higher level of
abstraction than used in LINPACK), he can clearly see that
properties related to separation of matrix elements in storage
are irrelevant to its correct functioning; indeed, they cannot even be formulated at this level of abstraction.   Thus,
one is assured that any other concrete program obtained from
this abstract one will be equally correct, even if it does
not have any storage separation properties.

One should note at this point that the idea of abstract
programming is not new.   It was the motivation behind the
development of extensible languages, including SIMULA 67,
Algol 68, and to some extent, PL/I.   Some of the advantages
of abstraction and stepwise refinement as a programming methodology are discussed by Wirth (1971), Cheatham and Wegbreit
(1972), and Bauer (1976).   The idea that abstraction will increase the adaptability of a program is at least implicit in
Parnas' work on information hiding [Parnas (1972)] and is
nicely discussed by Linden (1976).   Constructing the sequence
of programs in an adaptation semi-automatically or

automatically has been proposed only somewhat more recently;
Boyle (1977, 1979) discusses this idea for numerical software,
Burstall and Darlington (1977) discuss it for recursive pro-
grams, Barstow and Kant (1976) discuss such constructions in
the PSI program synthesis system [Green (1976)] and Balzer,
Goldman, and Wile (1976) discuss it in general; Partsch and
Broy (1979) discuss some of its theoretical foundations.

WHAT IS THE RANGE OF ADAPTATIONS OF AN ABSTRACT PROGRAM?

The discussion of the preceding section essentially answers this question, for it shows that the reliability-preserving adaptations considered here must preserve all properties
provable about the abstract prototype program from which they
begin. They may, of course, add properties, but one cannot
expect to obtain by such adaptations a program having properties which contradict those of the abstract program, even if
it is viewed as solving a "closely related problem."

Processes which derive programs with some related and
some contradictory properties I shall call *modifications*. It
seems that carrying them out must involve some human insight,
or what may be equivalent, selective application of transformations which do not preserve correctness in general. Nevertheless, the techniques which are useful in reliability-preserving adaptation, especially abstraction and transformation,
also assist in modifying software, as discussed by Belady
(1980) and Parnas (1976).

These observations also permit one to answer the question:
"Why not write just one abstract program, *compute*?" This
question is sometimes raised as a kind of reductio ad absurdum
argument against abstract programming, for presumably any program can be derived from *compute*. Unfortunately, no properties can be proved about it either, and thus no one would ever
select it to perform a computation.

Thus for any task there is an ideal level of abstraction:
the highest level of abstraction that still allows one to
prove the properties he requires of the program, i.e., that it
solves his problem. The program at this level in effect defines an equivalence class of programs, each member of which

solves the problem equally correctly. Usually, particular
members are chosen from this class on the basis of extra-
correctness concerns, such as efficiency.

HOW CAN ADAPTED PROGRAMS BE MADE EFFICIENT?

Efficiency, broadly interpreted, is the underlying motivation for considering reliability-preserving adaptations, since
in its absence one might as well just use the abstract prototype program (even though it may have zero efficiency, i.e.,
not be executable in the usual sense). In the discussion of
LINPACK adaptations, this motivation was reflected in questions of the form: "How can this program be simplified
(optimized) if I assume x?" That is, if one is willing to
add assumptions to the abstract prototype which restrict its
generality, can he then improve the efficiency of the program
by using these additional assumptions? One is thus led to
conclude that optimization is an essential part of any adaptation, for it would be foolhardy to sacrifice generality without gaining something from doing so.

The optimizations of use in adaptation can be characterized as propagating throughout the program the effect of the
highly-local assumptions added during adaptation; in the process they may replace these local assumptions by other, more
global but still consistent, ones. This process can be seen
in the adaptation of the LINPACK complex programs for use with
real data. The locally added assumption is that the imaginary
parts of all complex variables are zero for real data; in
FORTRAN notation, this corresponds to substituting 0.0E0 for
AIMAG(X) (for all X) wherever it occurs. Optimizations then
simplify the program. One of these is to change declarations
from COMPLEX to REAL, which saves storage. Others save computations; for example, the statement:

    IF (REAL(A(J,J)) .LE. 0.0E0 .OR. AIMAG(A(J,J)).NE. 0.0E0)
        . . .

which occurs in the Cholesky decomposition program to test for
a violation of the requirement of positive-definiteness, becomes successively:

```
--> IF (A(J,J) .LE. 0.0E0 .OR. 0.0E0 .NE. 0.0E0)...
--> IF (A(J,J) .LE. 0.0E0 .OR. .FALSE.)...
--> IF (A(J,J) .LE. 0.0E0)...
```

as the effect of the assumption is propagated. Similar, but often more global, propagations are a feature of all of the adaptations studied thus far.

This view of optimization also suggests that a further characterization of a program at the ideal level of abstraction for a given problem is that it is one which cannot be optimized. For it is supposed to embody all and only those assumptions necessary to prove that it solves the given problem; hence, none of these assumptions can be exchanged for a differing one without changing the properties of the abstract program. Assumptions which are added during adaptation, however, are candidates for exchange, since they cannot invalidate the properties of the abstract program.

It is thus clear that optimization is intimately related to adaptation, and one may expect that abstraction will benefit optimization in the same way it does adaptation. For much of the effort of classical program optimization is devoted to analyzing the apparent properties of the program to see if they are actually non-essential and can be exchanged for other, more preferred, ones. This is the same problem faced in trying to adapt an overly-concrete program, as discussed above. Thus it can be expected that optimization based on the abstract program will be much easier, much more secure, and much more effective than the usual approach.

Although a contrary view is espoused by Burstall and Darlington (1977), I believe such optimizations will turn out to be *domain-dependent* [i.e., to depend on a particular abstract data type, such as matrices, see Boyle (1979)] and perhaps even *representation-dependent* [i.e., to depend on a given concrete representation of an abstraction, see Boyle (1979)]. If this be true, it is important that it be easy to specify such optimizations together with the specification of abstract data types and their implementations.

HOW CAN PROGRAM ADAPTATION BE CARRIED OUT?

The above discussion of the role of optimization in the
LINPACK complex to real adaptation suggests why source-to-
source program transformation techniques [as discussed in
Boyle and Matz (1977); Loveman (1977); Bauer (1976); Burstall
and Darlington (1977); Arsac (1979); Balzer, Goldman, and
Wile (1978); and Boyle (1979)] are attractive for carrying
out program adaptations, for they provide a high-level notation for describing the context-dependent replacement of one
programming-language construct by another. For the LINPACK
example, the assumption-substituting transformations which
apply to arithmetic primaries are, in TAMPR notation [Boyle
and Matz (1977)]:

```
<primary>
{.SD. REAL(<expr>"l") ==> (<expr>"l") .SC.
 .SD. AIMAG(<expr>"l") ==> 0.0E0 .SC.
 .SD. CONJG(<expr>"l") ==> (<expr>"l") .SC.
}
```

plus some others for constants and for changing types in
declarations. The optimization transformations participating
in the example are:

```
<relation>
{.SD.
   <arith expr> "l" .NE. <arith expr> "l"
==>
   .FALSE.
.SC.}

<logical expr>
{.SD.
   <logical expr> "l" .OR. .FALSE.
==>
   <logical expr> "l"
.SC.}
```

In practice, additional transformations for other logical
operators, for other relational operators, for arithmetic
operators, etc., are also included.

A significant advantage of program transformations, which stems from their high-level, is that they constitute a single notation for describing both concrete implementations of abstract data and their optimization. Thus they offer the possibility that the designer of an abstract data structure and its implementation, who is in the best position to do so, can simultaneously specify its optimization. Further examples and details of such optimizations and their specification by transformations are discussed by Boyle (1979).

CONCLUSIONS

I have discussed some of the economic advantages of the use of reliability-preserving program adaptations as a software engineering program development strategy, and some of the research questions raised by attempting to do so. While not universally applicable (families of programs are not always required, and some areas of computer science are not well enough understood to enable their coding strategies to be formalized), these techniques nevertheless show considerable promise both for research and practice over the next decade. Moreover, their application on a modest scale in the development of LINPACK demonstrates that this promise is not only potential, but actual.

ACKNOWLEDGMENTS

The view of the role of adaptation in software engineering discussed here has been strongly influenced by discussions with Prof. Dr. F. L. Bauer and his project CIP; I am also indebted to him for arranging for my brief visit to the Technical University of Munich. It also benefited from numerous discussions with K. W. Dritz, W. M. Gentleman, B. S. Kerns, C. B. Moler, and B. T. Smith. Finally, I want to thank my aircraft draftsman, Judy Beumer, for actualizing the aircraft designs.

REFERENCES

Arsac, J. J. (Jan. 1979). Syntactic source to source transformation and program manipulation, *Comm. ACM 22(1)*, 43-54.
Backus, J. W. (Aug. 1978). Can programming be liberated from
  the von Neumann style? A functional style and its algebra
  of programs, *Comm. ACM 21(8)*, 613-641.
Balzer, R., Goldman, N., and Wile, D. (1976). On the trans-
  formational implementation approach to programming, *Proc.
  2nd Int'l. Conf. on Software Engineering*, San Francisco,
  337-344.
Barstow, D. R., and Kant, E. (1976). Observations on the in-
  teraction between coding and efficiency knowledge in the
  PSI program synthesis system, *Proc. 2nd Int'l. Conf. on
  Software Engineering*, San Francisco, 19-31.
Bauer, F. L. (1976). Programming as an evolutionary process,
  Proc. 2nd Int'l. Conf. on Software Engineering, San
  Francisco, 223-234.
Belady, L., and Leavenworth, B. M. (1980). Program modifia-
  bility, *In* "Software Engineering" (H. Freeman and P.
  Lewis, eds.), Academic Press, New York.
Boyle, J. M. (1977). Mathematical software transportability
  systems -- Have the variations a theme?, *In* "Portability
  of Numerical Software," Lecture Notes in Computer Science,
  No. 57, Springer-Verlag, 305-359.
Boyle, J. M. (March 1979). Extending reliability: transfor-
  mational tailoring of abstract mathematical software,
  SIGNUM conference on the Programming environment for de-
  velopment of numerical software, *SIGNUM Newsletter 14(1)*,
  57-60.
Boyle, J. M. (April 5-6, 1979). Program adaptation and pro-
  gram transformation, *In* "Proceedings of the Workshop on
  Softwareadaptation and Maintenance," (R. Ebert, J.
  Luegger, and R. Goecke, eds.), Elsevier-North Holland,
  Berlin.
Boyle, J. M., and Matz, M. (1977). Automating multiple pro-
  gram realizations, *In* "Proceedings of the MRI Symposium,
  XXIV: Computer Software Engineering," Polytechnic Press,
  421-456.

Burstall, R. M., and Darlington, J. A. (Jan. 1977). A transformation system for developing recursive programs, *J.
ACM 1*, 44-67.

Cheatham, T. E., and Wegbreit, B. (1972). A laboratory for
the study of automatic programming, *AFIPS Conf. Proc.
SJCC 1972 40*, 11-21.

Dongarra, J. J., and Hinds, A. R. (1979). Unrolling loops in
FORTRAN, *Software - Practice and Experience 9*, 219-226.

Dongarra, J. J., Bunch, J. R., Moler, C. B., and Stewart, G.
W. (1979). "LINPACK Users' Guide," SIAM, Philadelphia,
PA.

Green, C. C. (1976). The design of the PSI program synthesis
system, *Proc. 2nd Conf. on Software Engineering*, San
Francisco, 4-18.

Hague, S. J. (1978). Software tools, *In* "Numerical Software
-- Needs and Availability," (D. Jacobs, ed.), Academic
Press, New York, 57-79.

Lawson, C., Hanson, R., Kincaid, D., and Krogh, F. (1980).
Basic linear algebra subprograms for Fortran Usage, *ACM
Trans. Math. Software (to appear)*.

Linden, T. A. (1976). The use of abstract data types to
simplify program modifications, *SIGPLAN Notices 11*, 12-23
(Special Issue: Proceedings of Conference on Data:
Abstraction, Definition and Structure).

Loveman, D. B. (Jan. 1977). Program improvement by source
to source transformation, *J. ACM 24(1)*, 121-145.

Parnas, D. L. (March 1976). On the design and development of
program families, *IEEE Transactions on Software Engineering SE-2(1)*, 1-9.

Parnas, David L. (Dec. 1972). On the criteria to be used in
decomposing a system into modules, *Comm. ACM 15(12)*, 1053-
1058.

Partsch, H., and Broy, M. (1979). Examples for change of
types and object structures, *In* "Program Construction,"
(F. L. Bauer and M. Broy, eds.), Lecture Notes in Computer
Science No. 69, Springer Verlag.

Tsichritzis, D. (1980). The impact of technology on software,
In "Software Engineering," (H. Freeman and P. Lewis, eds.),
Academic Press, New York.

Wirth, N. (April 1971). Program development by stepwise
    refinement, *Comm. ACM 14(4)*, 221-227.

MY HOPES OF COMPUTING SCIENCE

Edsger W. Dijkstra

BURROUGHS

Nuenen, The Netherlands

Formulae have always frightened me. They frightened me,
I remember, when I was sixteen and had bought my books for
the next year. I was particularly alarmed by my new book on
trigonometry, full of sines, cosines, and Greek letters, and
asked my mother -- a gifted mathematician -- whether trigonometry was difficult. I gratefully acknowledge her wise
answer:

> "Oh no. Know your formulae, and always remember
> that you are on the wrong track when you need
> more than five lines."

In retrospect, I think that no other advice has had such a
profound influence on my way of working.

A quarter of a century later, formulae still frightened
me. When I saw Hoare's correctness proof of the procedure
"FIND" for the first time, I was horrified, and declared that
such a ballet of symbols was not my cup of tea.

And even now my first reaction to formulae, written by
someone else, is one of repulsion -- in particular when an
unfamiliar notational convention is used -- and when reading
an article, my natural reaction is to skip the formulae.

At the same time I have a warm appreciation for well-
designed formalisms that enable me to do things that I
couldn't possibly do without them. I acquired almost naturally

*© 1979 IEEE. Reprinted, with permission, from Proceedings,
4th International Conference on Software Engineering, September 17-19, 1979, Munich, Germany.*

© 1979 IEEE. Reprinted with permission,
from *Proc. 4th Int. Conf.* Software Engineering,
September 17-19, 1979, Munich, Germany.

my agility in the first-order predicate calculus like I had
learned trigonometry 25 years earlier, and in both cases using
the tool effectively gives me great intellectual satisfaction.

I can explain this love-hate relationship only in one way.
Why should I continue to shudder at the sight of formulae,
whereas in the meantime I should know better? I think that,
by now, I know from sad experience that only too many mathematicians and computing scientists have had the misfortune of
missing my mother's wise advice at the impressible age of sixteen. Too often the five-line limit is ignored and, instead
of using the compactness of the formal notation to keep the
text concise, authors use it -- in a still limited space! --
for the introduction of much more complexity than I feel com-
fortable with. Hence my shudder. (I don't know how you feel
about the famous Report on the Algorithmic Language ALGOL 60.
I admire it very much and think its fame well-deserved. But
in retrospect I think ALGOL 60's syntax, though rigorously
defined, more baroque than is desirable, and it is certainly
the compactness of BNF that has made the introduction of so
much arbitrariness possible.)

Later I learned that for the kind of effectiveness that I
loved, mathematicians had a perfectly adequate, technical
term: they call it "mathematical elegance" or "elegance" for
short. I also discovered that the term is much more "technical" than most mathematicians suspect, much more "technical"
in the sense that even among mathematicians of very different
brands there exists a much greater consensus about what is a
really elegant argument than they themselves seemed to be
aware of. Show any mathematician a really elegant argument
that is new for him: at the moment it becomes his intellectual property, he starts to laugh!

The discovery of this strong consensus has made a great
impression on me. It was very encouraging. It came at a moment that -- in private, so to speak -- I had already come to
the conclusion that in the practice of computing, where we
have so much latitude for making a mess of it, mathematical
elegance is not a dispensable luxury, but a matter of life and
death. But I hesitated to say so very much in public, just
for fear of pushing another buzz-word; now I dare to do it,

assured as I am that mathematical elegance is a clear notion,
firmly rooted in our culture. But I am also aware of the fact
that my sensitivity for it can be tracked down to how I was
educated in my youth.

Language is another issue. I often feel uneasy about it.
At the time I got my mother's wise advice about trigonometry,
I wrote many poems, and often I was dissatisfied: I knew
that what I had written was not "it", yet I found myself unable to identify the shortcoming, and had to console myself
with A. A. Milne's "As near as you can get nowadays.".

My first task at the Mathematical Centre in Amsterdam was
writing the precise functional specification for the computer
that was there at that moment under design. I did so to the
best of my ability, and thought I had done so rather well --
and, from the point of precision, I had --. But it was something of a shock for me to discover that, within a few days
after its appearance, my beautiful report was generally known
as "The Appalling Prose".

At that time I only felt that we had to learn how to
write better about our own subject. I think that it was not
until 1960, when Peter Naur acquainted me with Wittgenstein's
famous quotation:

> "What can be said at all, can be said clearly;
> and on what we cannot talk about, we have to
> remain silent."

that it slowly dawned upon me that, therefore, we had to learn
how to *think* better about our own subject.

In the meantime I had had another linguistic shock: I
became a member of the ACM, shortly before its Communications
started to appear. Prior to that I had hardly had any exposure to the foreign literature. What I then read was written
in a way so totally different from what I, in relative isolation, had acquired as my own habit, that I was absolutely
flabbergasted. The heavily anthropomorphic terminology was
totally new for me, and hardly compatible with my cultural
roots; so was the animism betrayed by the term "bug": we had
never called a bug a bug, we had always called it an error.

Still hesitating whether or not to adopt the jargon, I
was confronted with a next term of a glaring inadequacy

-- was it "program maintenance"? I don't remember -- and I
knew that I had to design my own way of writing about our
subject in English, as I had done in Dutch. In retrospect
this may strike you as a proud decision, but it wasn't: it
was a decision taken in desperation, for otherwise I could
not think in the way I wished to think.

One more remark about language that seems relevant. With
English being computing science's Esperanto, colleagues with
English as their native tongue often feel somewhat quilty
about what they regard as their undeserved advantage over most
foreigners. Their feeling of guilt is misplaced, because the
advantage is ours. It is very helpful to have to do your work
in what always remains a foreign language, as it forces you
to express yourself more consciously. (About the most excellent prose written in our field that I can think of, is to be
found in the aforementioned ALGOL 60 Report: its editor had
the great advantage of being, besides brilliant, a Dane. I
have always felt that much of the stability and well-deserved
fame of ALGOL 60 could be traced down directly to the inexor-
able accuracy of Peter Naur's English.)

The above has been presented, by way of background information, as a help for the interpretation of what follows: a
summary of my hopes of computing science. This topic is not
as frivolous as it might seem at first sight. Firstly,
already in my early youth -- from 1940 until 1945 -- I have
learned to hope very seriously; secondly, my hopes of computing science -- which have directed most of my work -- have
shown a great stability. They evolved: some hopes became
fulfilled, some hopes, originally far away, became almost
challenges as their fulfillment began to appear technically
feasible. Admittedly they are only my hopes, but they are of
a sufficiently long standing that I now dare to confess them.

How were we attracted to the field of automatic computing?
Why do we remain fascinated? What is really the core of computing science?

Well, everybody got attracted in his or her way. I
entered the field by accident. I became attracted by the combination of the urgency of the problems that needed to be
solved for the recovery of my country from the damage done

to it in World War II, and the discovery that carefully applied brains were an essential ingredient of the solutions. Up till that moment I had never been quite sure whether my love of perfection had been a virtue or a weakness, and I was greatly relieved to find an environment in which it was an indispensable virtue.

I became -- and remained -- fascinated by the amazing combination of simplicity and complexity. On the one hand it is a trivial world, being built from a finite number of noughts and ones, so trivial that one feels oneself mathematically entitled, and hence morally obliged, to complete intellectual mastery. On the other hand it has shown itself to be a world of treacherous complexity. The task that should be possible, but wasn't, became the fascinating challenge.

For me, the first challenge for computing science is to discover how to maintain order in a finite, but very large, discrete universe that is intricately intertwined. And a second, but not less important challenge is how to mould what you have achieved in solving the first problem, into a teachable discipline: it does not suffice to hone your own intellect (that will join you in your grave), you must teach others how to hone theirs. The more you concentrate on these two challenges, the clearer you will see that they are only two sides of the same coin: teaching yourself is discovering what is teachable.

As I said, my hopes have evolved, and one way in which they did so was by becoming more precise and more articulate. Ten years ago I expressed my dissatisfaction with the then current state of the art by aiming at programs that would be "intellectually manageable" and "understandable". At the time they represented the best way in which I could express my then still vague hope; I apologize for these terms to the extent that they became buzz-words before they had become sufficiently precise to be technically helpful. What does it help to strive for "intellectual manageability" when you don't know how you would prefer to "manage intellectually"? What guidance do you get from the goal of "understandability" before you have chosen the way of understanding? Very little, of course.

I particularly regret my use of the term "understanding",
for in the combination "ease of understanding" it has added
to the confusion by *not* inviting to distinguish carefully between "convenient" and "conventional", and that distinction,
I am afraid, is vital: I expect for computing scientists the
most convenient way of thinking and understanding to be
rather *un*conventional. (That is not surprising at all, for,
after all, also thinking is only a habit, and what right do
we have to expect our old habits to be adequate when faced,
for the first time in our culture, with a drastically novel
universe of discourse?)

My hope became more articulate, when programming emerged
as an application area par excellence of the techniques of
scientific thought, techniques that are well-known because we
struggle with the small sizes of our heads as long as we
exist. They are roughly of three different forms:

1) separation of concerns and effective use of abstraction
2) the design and use of notations, tailored to one's manipu-
    lative needs.
3) avoiding case analyses, in particular combinatorially
    exploding ones.

When faced with an existing design, you can apply them as a
checklist; when designing yourself, they provide you with
strong heuristic guidance. In my experience they make the
goal "intellectually manageable" sufficiently precise to be
actually helpful, in a degree that ranges from "very" to
"extremely so".

For the techniques of scientific thought I called programming an application area "par excellence", and with that last
term I meant two things: indispensable and very effective.

That they are indispensable seems obvious to me. They
summarize the only ways in which we have ever been able to
disentangle complexity more or less successfully; and we cannot expect our designs to turn out to be any better than the
ways in which we have thought about them, for that would be a
miracle. The indispensability of the techniques of scientific
thought is, admittedly, only my belief, and you are free to

dismiss it; you could remark that I am primarily a scientist
and that to someone, whose only tool is a hammer, every problem looks like a nail.

I am, however, strengthened in my belief of their indispensability by the outcome of the experiments that we could
take, viz. trying how effectively we could learn to apply the
techniques of scientific thought. Of the experiments I am
aware of, the outcome has been very encouraging. Engaged in
these experiments, you start to treasure the just solvable
problems, and try to present the most elegant solution you can
think of as nicely as possible. I have now joined that game
for several years and cannot recommend it warmly enough. It
is a highly rewarding and fascinating learning process.

It is very rewarding for its immediate benefit: a significant decrease in the average amount of effort, needed to
find a solution. The untrained thinker -- unless a genius --
spends inordinate amounts of effort in avoidable complications,
and only too often, unaware of their avoidability, he fails to
disentangle himself again: a vast amount of effort has then
been spent on producing an inferior solution.

Our educators have something to answer for. Reading the
literature, I must come to the sad conclusion, that untrained
thinkers are rather the rule than the exception: people have
been taught facts and tricks, but not a methodology for using
their brains effectively.

The scope of the educational challenge is enormous. If
you accept it -- and I think we should -- you have my blessing.
You'll need it -- and much more! -- because you will encounter
formidable obstacles on your way. You'll have at least two
dragons to slay. Confusing "love of perfection" with "claim
of perfection", people will accuse you of the latter and then
blame you for the first. Furthermore, in spite of all the
evidence to the contrary, the teachability of thinking effectively will be flatly denied, and your methodological contributions -- needed more than anything else -- will be dismissed
as "for geniuses only": remember, while fighting this second
dragon, that most frequently the term "genius" is not used as
a compliment, but only as an alibi for the mentally lazy.

For a prosperous future of computing science -- like for
any science -- it is essential that its achievements are published well, so that the next generation can start where the
preceding one left. Above, I have expressed some of my dissatisfaction about the quality of today's publications in our
field. The problem is a very serious one, and it is more than
a purely educational problem. How do we publish a sophisticated piece of software? (We can reproduce the code, but that
is only fit for mechanical execution. I meant "to publish" in
the scientific sense: our text should fully enlighten the
attentive reader.) Admittedly, many papers about algorithms
could be written much better already now, but beyond a certain
limit, no one knows for certain, how to do it well! And that
universal inability makes it a technical problem, urgent and
as yet unsolved. One of my fervent hopes is that we shall
solve it.

How should a well-written publication about a sophisticated piece of software look like? We don't know yet, but two
things seem certain. Firstly, the texts will be "mathematical"
in the sense of Morris Kline, when he wrote:

"More than anything else mathematics is a method."

Secondly, the texts will have to be written in a style that is
very different from the style of traditional mathematical
texts. Depending on your mood you may regard this either as
disturbing or as exciting, but in any case you should be con-
vinced of the necessity of developing a radically new style
of writing mathematical texts, very unlike anything ever
written before: this novelty is required by the novelty of
the subject matter. Traditionally, mathematical texts are
written on a fairly uniform semantic level, and that style
cannot suffice for the disentanglement of the many intricate
intertwinings we have to deal with.

In the relation between mathematics and computing science,
the latter has, up till now, mostly been at the receiving end,
and it seems to me that the time has come to start repaying
our debts. Besides broadening the scope of applicability of
mathematical techniques (as indicated above) we could also
change their traditional applications. When, at last, the
predicate calculus were to become an indispensable tool in the

daily reasoning of all sorts of mathematicians, when the replacement of the asymmetric implication by the symmetric dis-
junction were to rob the so-called "reductio ad absurdum" from
its special status and equivalence would no longer be expressed by the clumsy "if and only if", when mathematics would
become enriched by a greater variety of inductive arguments,
in all those cases such a development could possibly be traced
down to computing science's wholesome influence.

But repaying our debt to mathematics at large is certainly
not our only task: also computing proper needs our attention.
We know that the problems of programming and system design are
such that they cannot be solved without an effective application of the techniques of scientific thought. But how well
are we able to apply them?

How well are we, for instance able to separate the concern
for correctness from the concern for efficiency? Both concerns are so "major", that I don't believe that significant
progress will be possible unless we manage to separate them
completely.

Efficiency has to do with cost aspects of program execution, correctness has to do with a relation between input and
output, between initial and final states. Complete separation
of these two concerns means that we can deal with the correctness issue without taking into account that our programs could
be executed. It means that we can deal with the correctness
issue, temporarily ignoring that our program text also admits
the interpretation of executable code, i.e., we *must* be able
to discuss correctness independently of any underlying computational model. To learn to dissociate our reasoning from
underlying computational models, and to get rid of our operational models, and to get rid of our operational thinking
habits, that is what I regard as computing science's major
task. That is what I would like to see achieved more than
anything else.

Its difficulty should not be underestimated: it is like
asking the average mathematician suddenly to do Euclidean geometry without drawing pictures. As Morris Kline remarks:

"But the pictures are not the subject matter of
geometry and we are not permitted to reason from
them. It is true that most people including
mathematicians, lean upon these pictures as a
crutch and find themselves unable to walk when
the crutch is removed. For a tour of higher
dimensional geometry, however, the crutch is not
available."

The anology is almost perfect: the pictures are to geometry
what computational histories (or "traces") are to computing
science, "and we are not permitted to reason from them". But
the operational thinking habits are firmly rooted in many
wide-spread traditions, ranging from automata theory, via
LISP, to FORTRAN and BASIC, and many people, including computing scientists, lean upon traces "as a crutch, and find
themselves unable to walk when the crutch is removed". In
the case of uniprogramming the trace is a linear sequence of
states and events, about as manageable and "helpful" as a
picture in two- or three-dimensional geometry. But in the
case of multiprogramming traces are unmanageable and "the
crutch is not available".

For Euclidean geometry the analytical methods of Descartes
provided the alternative to the crutch, and in analytical
geometry the generalization from three to more dimensions was
technically very smooth. In programming, the postulational
methods of Floyd and Hoare provided the alternative to the
crutch; in uniprogramming they did so very successfully, but
their generalization from uni- to multiprogramming is -- at
the time of writing and to my knowledge -- less smooth,
although after the successful start of Gries and Owicki I
haven't the slightest doubt that in the long run it will be
done quite successfully. The need to delineate very carefully
one's "point actions" is a new aspect of the game; so is the
discovery of Laws that give the implementer a greater freedom
in embedding in space and time the activities involved in the
implementation of single point actions. (One of the ways in
which we can appreciate the manifestly greater difficulty of
designing multiprograms is that the implementer is interested
in much greater freedom: under which circumstances, for

instance, is he allowed to implement in a distributed system a point action -- in the presence of other traffic! -- by an activity in node A, followed by a "slow" message from A to B, and finally, upon reception of the message, some activity in B?)

Dealing successfully with these technicalities will, I am very much afraid, be a minor task, compared to the educational challenge of getting nonoperational arguments accepted and getting people thereby out of their operational thinking habits, for over and over again they prove to be a mental stumbling block for accepting a nonoperational argument, particularly when, from an operational point of view, it does not make sense. It is distressingly hard to make someone accept a universal invariant while *he* all the time remains obsessed by *his* knowledge that in *his* implementation it will *never* be true, because his implementation will never show a moment in which it won't be halfway engaged on one or more point actions somewhere in the network. The fight against operational thinking habits is a major educational task (of which the crusade against anthropomorphic terminology is only a modest beginning.)

I hope very much that computing science at large will become more mature, as I am annoyed by two phenomena that both strike me as symptoms of immaturity.

The one is the wide-spread sensitivity to fads and fashions, and the wholesale adoption of buzz-words and even buzz-notions. Write a paper promising salvation, make it a "structured" something or a "virtual" something, or "abstract", "distributed" or "higher-order" or "applicative" and you can almost be certain of having started a new cult.

The other one is the sensitivity to the market place, the unchallenged assumption that industrial products, just because they are there, become by their mere existence a topic worthy of scientific attention, no matter how grave the mistakes they embody. In the sixties the battle that was needed to prevent computing science from degenerating to "how to live with the 360" has been won, and "courses" -- usually "in depth"! -- about MVS or what have you are now confined to the not so respectable subculture of the commercial training circuit.

But now we hear that the advent of the microprocessors is
going to revolutionize computing science! I don't believe
that, unless the chasing of day-flies is confused with doing
research. A similar battle may be needed.

An unmistakable symptom of maturity of computing science
would be a consensus about "what matters" among its leaders,
a consensus that would enable us to discuss its future course
as if computing science were an end in itself. Obviously,
such a consensus can only emerge as the byproduct of a coherent body of knowledge and insights, but the crucial point
is "knowledge of what?" and "insights in what?". What would
be worth knowing? What would be worth understanding?

I believe that a bold extrapolation from the past will
help us to find the answers. When programming methodology in
the early seventies adopted formal techniques for verification
and for the derivation of correct programs, earlier ways in
which programming language features had been discussed were
suddenly obsolete. The earlier pragmatic discussions, blurred
by different tastes and habits, had only created a confusion
worthy of Babel, but then the simple question "does this proposed feature simplify or complicate a formal treatment?" cut
as a knife through the proposals and did more to establish
consensus than eloquence or bribery could ever have achieved.
My extrapolation from that experience is that our knowledge
should concern formal techniques, and our understanding should
be of the limits and of the potential of their application.

Let me comment in this connection shortly on two developments currently in bloom, developments that certainly fall
under the heading "formal techniques": the knowledge is being
developed, but about the understanding of limits and potential
I have in both cases my misgivings. I mean abstract data
types and program transformation, both under development in
an effort to separate correctness concerns from efficiency
concerns.

For the blooming of abstract data types I feel some co-
responsibility, having coined and launched the term "representational abstraction" back in 1972, and if it turns out to
be a mistake, part of the guilt could be mine. One hint that
it might be a mistake comes from the fact that it is only a

slight exaggeration to state that, after five years of inten-
sive research and development, the stack is still the only
abstract data type ever designed. This is in strong contrast
to what happened when its inspirator, the closed subroutine,
was invented! For this disappointing outcome, so far, of the
research devoted to abstract data types I can, at my current
stage of understanding, offer two tentative explanations. The
one is simply that an abstract data type is so much more complicated, so much harder to specify, than a subroutine, that
it is orders of magnitude harder to invent a useful one. (If
that is the case, I have only been impatient.) The other one
is that, when all is said and told, the type of interface, as
provided by an abstract data type, is inappropriate for its
purpose: when we analyze carefully really sophisticated algorithms, we could very well discover that the correctness proof
does *not* admit a parcelling out, such that one or two parcels
can comfortably be identified with an abstract data type. In
other words, the hope that abstract data types will help us
much could very well be based on an underestimation of the
logical complexity of sophisticated algorithms and, consequently, on an oversimplification of the program design process.

Program transformations -- each of which embodies a theorem! -- have been suggested as a candidate that could contribute to the necessary body of knowledge. The hope is that
transformations from a modest library will provide a path
from a naive, inefficient, but obviously correct program to a
sophisticated efficient solution. I have seen how via program
transformations striking gains in efficiency have been obtained by avoiding recomputations of the same intermediate
results, even in situations in which this possibility -- note
that the intermediate results are never part of the original
problem statement! -- was, at first sight, surprising. And
yet my hope is tempered for the following reason: when, in
contrast to the correctness of the naive algorithm one starts
with, the correctness of the efficient one critically depends
on a (perhaps deep) mathematical theorem, the chain of transformations would constitute a proof of the latter, and, to the
best of my knowledge, mechanical proof verification is very

cumbersome and is expected to remain so. I am afraid that
great hopes of program transformations can only be based on
what seems to me an underestimation of the logical brinkman-
ship that is required for the justification of really efficient algorithms. It is certainly true, that each program
transformation embodies a theorem, but are these the theorems
that could contribute significantly to the body of knowledge
and understanding that would give us maturity? I doubt it,
for many of them are too trivial and too much tied to program
notation.

And this brings me to my final hope: before I die, I hope
to understand by which virtues the one formal notational technique serves its purpose well and due to which shortcomings
the other one is just a pain in the neck.

On my many wanderings over the earth's surface I learned
that quite a few people tend to help me starting an animated
conversation by the well-intended question: "And, professor
Dijkstra, what are you currently researching?". I have
learned to dread that question, because it used to leave me
speechless, or stammering at best. Came the moment that I
decided that I had better design a ready-made answer for it,
and for a while I used the answer, both true and short:
"Programming.". The usual answer I got was very illuminating
"Ah, I see: programming languages.", and when I then said
"No: programming.", my good-willing partner seldomly noticed
that he was being corrected.

The ACM has a Special Interest Group on Programming Languages, but *not* one on programming as such; its newest peri-
odical is on Programming Languages and Systems and *not* on
programming as such. The computing community has an almost
morbid fixation on program notation, it is subdivided in as
many subcultures as we have more or less accepted programming
languages, subcultures, none of which clearly distinguishes
between genuine problems and problems only generated by the
programming language it has adopted (sometimes almost as a
faith). For this morbid fixation I can only offer one explanation: we fully realize that in our work, more than perhaps
anywhere else, appropriate notational conventions are crucial,
but also: we suffer more than anyone else from the general
misunderstanding of their proper role.

The problem is, of course, quite general: each experienced mathematician knows that achievements depend critically on the availability of suitable notations. Naively one would therefore expect that the design of suitable notations would be a central topic of mathematical methodology. Amazingly enough, the traditional mathematical world hardly addresses the topic. The clumsy notational conventions adhered to in many mathematical publications leave room for only one conclusion: mathematicians are not even taught how to select a suitable notation from the established ones, let alone that they are taught how to design a new one when needed.

This amazing silence of the mathematicians on what is at the heart of their trade suggests that it is a very tough job to say something sensible about it. (Otherwise they would have done it.) And I can explain it only by the fact that the traditional mathematician has always the escape of natural language with which he can glue his formulae together.

Here, the computing scientist is in a unique position, for a program text is, by definition, for one hundred percent a formal text. As a result we just cannot afford not to understand why a notational convention is appropriate or not. Such is our predicament.

TOOLS FOR THE EFFICIENT DESIGN OF SOFTWARE

M. David Freedman

Bendix Engineering Development Center
Southfield, Michigan
and
University of Michigan-Dearborn
Dearborn, Michigan

INTRODUCTION

During the past decade or so, the computer science community has realized that the development of software must be
upgraded from an art to an engineering science. As a result,
methodologies such as structured programming have emerged and
been developed. Additionally, many practitioners have begun
to think in terms of how to design software (as opposed to
how to code programs), and several software design methodologies now exist.

The proliferation of the microcomputer in the past few
years has caused the number of engineers who develop software
to increase at an unprecedented rate. Moreover, the low cost
of microcomputer hardware now contrasts sharply with the relatively high cost of the software being developed for these
systems. Thus, the software design methodologies should be
especially useful to the engineer who designs microcomputer
software. Unfortunately, many engineers are either unaware
of the existence of these methodologies or not sufficiently
trained to be able to use them. In fact, many engineers today

---

Portions of this article have been taken from: M. David
Freedman and Lansing B. Evans, *"Designing with Microcomputers:
A Systematic Approach,"* a forthcoming Prentice-Hall, Inc.
publication. *Reprinted by permission of Prentice-Hall, Inc.,
Englewood Cliffs, New Jersey.*

111

are being taught to develop software using techniques which
are over twenty years old. They program microcomputers in
machine code or assembly language, since they are taught that
compilers are "complicated and expensive" to use.

What the software designer needs is a design methodology
which he can understand and with which he can easily work.
To achieve the latter objective, we need to provide a set of
software design "tools" which contribute to the effective use
of the design methodology.

METHODOLOGY

Properties

A viable design methodology will enable the engineer to
produce software designs (and ultimately executable codes)
which will have the following properties:

1. Be of low complexity
2. Be easily understood
3. Be easily documented
4. Have a high probability of being correct
5. Be easily modified and maintained

The methodology itself should have the following properties:

1. Be easy to use and understand
2. Be easy to document
3. Provide work (and thereby cost) reduction

Thus the methodology should include the use of the following:

1. Top-down design
2. Modularity
3. Design language
4. Documentation

Top-Down Design

The design should be partitioned into different functional
levels. At the top level which is completed first, the design
should be the most general; at the bottom level it should be

the most detailed. This approach allows the design to proceed from the abstract at the top to the specific at the
bottom in a natural systematic way.

Modularity

All system functions which belong together or which manipulate a common data structure should be placed into a
single module. This provides a way of systematically designing the system. It also provides for control of access to
each data structure since only the procedures which are in a
particular module have access to the data structure within
that module. Each module should be broken down into procedures so that each procedure implements only a single function, if possible.

DESIGN LANGUAGE

Characteristics

The design language should consist of natural language
which has been embedded into a language which includes a small
number of "programming" constructs such as:

1. Do, Do while, etc., for loops
2. If...then...else..., for conditional tests
3. Call, Return, for control and to facilitate modularity

An example of a design language procedure is shown below:

```
PROCEDURE:  SEARCH (RECORD LIST, SEARCH KEY; FOUND RECORD)
BEGIN PROCEDURE
  DO FOR EACH RECORD IN RECORD LIST
    IF SEARCH KEY MATCHES KEY IN RECORD
      THEN  DO
              PUT RECORD WITH MATCHING KEY INTO FOUND RECORD
              RETURN
            END
  END
END PROCEDURE
```

As shown in the example above, the design language should
also have provision for specifying interprocedure parameters

clearly and unambiguously. In the example, the input parameters are RECORD LIST and SEARCH KEY; the output parameter is
FOUND RECORD.

The execution of the procedure is invoked by using a
calling sequence of the form:

CALL: SEARCH (RECORD LIST, SEARCH KEY; FOUND RECORD)

Documentation

The design language version of the system design provides
a high degree of visibility into the system. When combined
with module documentation and additional information (creation date, designer's name, modification dates, etc.) which
were omitted in the example above, the design language provides a basis for the next level of documentation, the coding
level. When the code is generated, it should be *inserted*
between the lines of the design language in a one-to-one (or
one-to-many) fashion.

The design language statements then become comments for
the code, are maintained with the code, and provide complete
documentation at the coding level. An example of the SEARCH
procedure using PL/M (which is a subset of PL/I) as the target
programming language is shown in Figure 1.

TOOLS

Currently there are tools available to aid in the production of machine readable code (editors), to translate source
code into machine code and find syntax errors (compilers,
assemblers), and to help find errors in the executable code
(debuggers). However, tools for creating, modifying and documenting the *design*, and for finding errors at the design level
are almost nonexistent. What we are developing is a set of
tools -- described below in terms of their functions -- to
fill this void.

1. *Design Preparation* - This tool is used to create
the design language version of each procedure, a
description of each module, and all other design
level documentation. It establishes the format

```
SEARCH:  DO;
/*  PROCEDURE:  SEARCH (RECORD LIST, SEARCH KEY; FOUND RECORD)                    */
                SEARCH:  PROCEDURE (RECORD$LIST$POINTER,SEARCH$KEY) ADDRESS;
/**************************************************************************************/
/*  DESIGNED BY:        M. D. FREEDMAN              4/4/79                          */
/*  REVISED BY:         M. D. FREEDMAN              5/8/79                          */
/*  MODULE:             MAINTAIN RECORD LIST                                        */
/*  CALLED BY:          PROCESS REQUEST                                            */
/*  PARAMETERS:         RECORD LIST   -   DATA LIST TO BE SEARCHED                  */
/*                      SEARCH KEY    -   KEY TO BE SEARCHED FOR                    */
/*                      FOUND RECORD  -   RECORD WHOSE KEY MATCHED SEARCH KEY       */
/**************************************************************************************/
/*  PROCEDURE DECLARATIONS                                                          */
                DECLARE (RECORD$LIST$POINTER,RECORD$POINTER) ADDRESS;
                DECLARE RECORD$LIST BASED RECORD$LIST$POINTER (128) STRUCTURE
                                            (KEY BYTE, VALUE (1Ø) ADDRESS);
                DECLARE (SEARCH$KEY,INDEX,COUNTER) BYTE;
                DECLARE RECORD STRUCTURE (KEY BYTE,VALUE (1Ø) ADDRESS);
/*  BEGIN PROCEDURE                                                                 */
/*    DO FOR EACH RECORD IN RECORD LIST                                             */
                        DO INDEX = Ø TO 127;
/*      IF SEARCH KEY MATCHES KEY IN RECORD                                         */
                        IF SEARCH$KEY = RECORD$LIST(INDEX).KEY
/*        THEN  DO                                                                  */
                                THEN  DO;
/*          PUT RECORD WITH MATCHING KEY INTO FOUND RECORD                          */
                                RECORD.KEY = RECORD$LIST(INDEX).KEY;
                                DO COUNTER = Ø TO 9;
                                  RECORD.VALUE(COUNTER) =
                                  RECORD$LIST(INDEX).VALUE(COUNTER);
                                END;
/*          RETURN                                                                  */
                                RECORD$POINTER = . RECORD;
                                RETURN RECORD$POINTER;
/*          END                                                                     */
                                END;
/*      END                                                                         */
                        END;
                END SEARCH;
/*  END PROCEDURE                                                                   */
END SEARCH;
```

FIGURE 1.   Example of the SEARCH procedure using PL/M.

of the documentation and easily provides for
"filling in the blanks" using function keys as
opposed to character-by-character typing. It
also establishes consistent indentation of the
design language constructs. Examples of function keys are:

>   Insert Header
>   Insert DO FOR EACH
>   .
>   .
>   .
>   END
>   Insert IF...
>   THEN
>   .
>   .
>   ELSE

When the header is inserted into the text, documentation information such as the designer's
name and the current date are automatically inserted into the header.

2. *Emulation* - This tool permits the software de-
    signer to "walkthrough" his design so that the
    control logic of the design can be verified.
    It can also provide a data flow diagram for each
    emulation. The emulator starts by stepping
    through the EXECUTIVE procedure. Whenever it
    encounters a CALL to another procedure, it
    automatically steps through the called proce-
    dure. When a RETURN is encountered, it returns
    to the calling procedure and continues to step
    through it. Since "walking through" the design
    does not entail the execution of any instruc-
    tions, the emulator has no way of evaluating
    whether a test condition is true or not. Thus,
    whenever a DO WHILE or IF statement is encoun-
    tered, the operator must indicate which course
    of action to take. One of the features built
    into the emulator is the ability to save the
    system state at any time so that the alternative
    course of action from the saved state can be
    taken at a later time. Although it is impossible

to exhaustively test a design during a walk-through, the emulator does provide a satisfac-tory way of ensuring that sequencing errors are minimized. As a result, a higher level of confidence in the correctness of the design can be achieved.

3. *Language Conversion* - This tool automatically converts as much of the design as possible to code. Design language statements are first con-verted to comments. Then, where possible, the programming language construct corresponding to the design language statement is generated and inserted into the text. For example, the DO FOREVER design language construct can be con-verting into the PL/M construct DO WHILE 1=1;. The code for the part of the design which can-not be converted automatically can be inserted by the designer using efficient function key entry mechanisms provided by the converter. Declarations can be inserted automatically where needed.

4. *Modification* - This text-editor like tool permits either the design language or the code to be changed easily. Indentation is preserved auto-matically in the presence of change, and consis-tency between the code and the design language is enforced. The latter is accomplished by keep-ing track of all changes made during an editing session. Then, for each case where a design language statement has been altered but not the corresponding programming language statement, or vice versa, the designer is asked to verify that the lack of change was intentional.

5. *Visual Aids* - This tool provides an easily visu-alizable description of the system. For example, the system modularization and the procedure call-ing tree, with or without parameter and data structure information, can be produced automatically

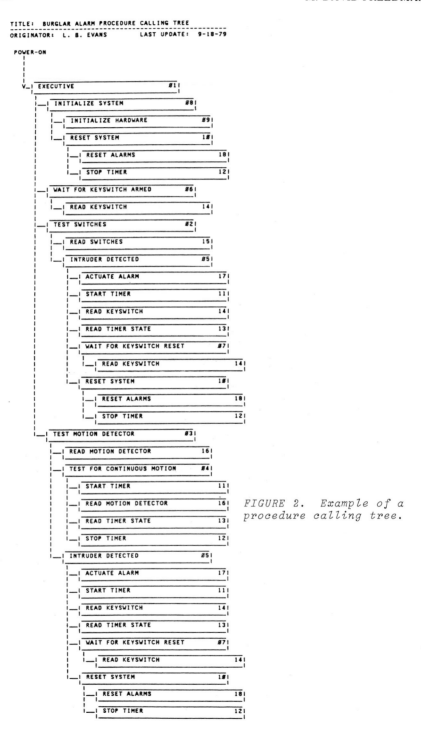

FIGURE 2. Example of a procedure calling tree.

to illustrate the relationship of the system
parts to each other. An example of a procedure
calling tree is shown in Figure 2.

ACKNOWLEDGMENTS

Support for development of the methodology has come from
both the University of Michigan-Dearborn and The Bendix
Corporation. Teaching of the methodology at the University
is also supported in part by the National Science Foundation.
The development of the tools is being supported by Bendix.

THE CENTRAL ROLE OF DESIGN
IN SOFTWARE ENGINEERING:
Implications for Research

Peter Freeman

University of California
Irvine, California

INTRODUCTION

In a previous paper [Freeman (1976)] I argued that the
design process should be viewed as the central, unifying activity of software engineering. If one is doing a requirements analysis to support a planned software development,
careful concern of design constraints must take place; if the
detailed technical specification of a system is being done,
then one is working directly with design features; and if one
is helping an existing software system evolve, then the design rationale on which it is based must be understood.   In
all of these software engineering activities, one is either
directly designing or is forced to deal with various aspects
of design. Thus the underlying assumption of my remarks is
that the design process plays a central role in software engineering.

Given then that design plays a central role in software
engineering (a point that I think most people will agree with),
there should be little argument ·that we should if possible try
to improve it through appropriate research. My central thesis
is that such improvement is possible if we have a solid
scientific understanding of design on which to build a viable
(software) engineering design methodology.

Essentially, we must have a body of teachable knowledge
about design. It should be intellectually rigorous, analytic,

formalized where appropriate, and based on empirical studies where possible. It is this kind of scientific understanding of physical phenomena that makes engineering in other disciplines possible. The "artificial" nature of software highlights the processes that create it and it is this situation that increases the importance of the design process in software engineering.

WHAT IS A SCIENCE OF DESIGN?

The central thesis of this article is based on the ideas of H. A. Simon, whose *Sciences of the Artificial* [Simon (1969)] should be required reading for anyone involved with software engineering. Professor Simon argues that our modern world has several very important undertakings that are wholly "artificial" (in the sense of being created by human beings), but that can be studied in a scientific manner. Computing is one of these.

Professor Simon also argues that modern engineering schools (and by implication, the research they support) have emphasized the natural science component of engineering to the exclusion of the study of design. In this context, he argues for the creation of a science of design to support engineering design in all fields.

He discusses seven components of a science of design:

- *the theory of evaluation that provides a framework for choice among given alternatives*
- *computational methods for actually making choices*
- *a formal logic to handle the "shoulds" of design*
- *search methods for finding alternatives*
- *the allocation of design resources*
- *theory of structure and design organization*
- *design representation*

Each of these topics is explained in more detail in his book.

In the context of software engineering, I have modified this list somewhat to include the following topics:

- *generation and selection of design alternatives*
- *design representations*
- *solution procedures for design problems*
- *how people design*
- *design structures*

These are the categories in the design area in which we can and should support research to strengthen software engineering. In the next section I will elaborate briefly on each of them.

AREAS FOR DESIGN RESEARCH

The following is a list of suggested areas for design research. The list is not intended to be exhaustive, nor are the areas explained in full detail. The objective here is only to indicate possible directions for research.

Generation and Selection of Alternatives

Design is sometimes conceptualized as a process of choosing among alternative structures (both gross and detailed) that go to make up the artifact being designed. This model of design implies that alternatives must be generated first, then evaluated, and finally one of them must be chosen. Some of the questions of interest for software design include:

- *How can spaces of alternatives be characterized in a well-defined way so that alternatives can be easily generated?*
- *How do we measure the quality of a design so that competing choices can be evaluated?*
- *How does the order in which design decisions are made limit or expand our options?*
- *Given a specific design problem, how can we allocate our resources in order to achieve a satisfactory design?*

Currently there is very little research that touches on this area. A few studies of software quality [e.g., Boehm *et al.* (1973)] and work on design complexity [e.g., McCabe

(1976)] provide us with some design metrics but there is almost no work on spaces of alternatives or design strategies.

A number of design methods are being proposed and some
of these [e.g., Yourdon and Constantine (1979)] explicitly
address some of the evaluation questions suggested above.
Most design methods, of course, are intended to be improved
means of generating and selecting alternatives. The problem,
however, is that they are not based on any scientific understanding of either the design process or the artifacts being
designed. Thus any improvements over intuitive design that
they may offer will come about through the natural percep-
tiveness of their inventors. While in fact many advances do
come about this way, in the long run, a science-based technology must depend on a solid basis of systematic knowledge.

Design Representations

The working representations of an engineered product (e.g.,
sketches, blueprints, diagrams, models) are important in any
field. In the software field, they are essential since the
artifact being designed and built exists in no other medium.

The fact that the representation of a problem effects
the ability of a person to solve that problem is well understood and relevant. Since design is essentially a problem-
solving exercise, the importance of representation to the design process is clear.

Some of the questions that need answers include:

- *What information is necessary to each stage of
  design?*
- *How can the information be represented to make
  it easy to determine properties of the design
  (e.g., completeness, quality, consistency)?*
- *How can the representation be used to help determine ramifications of the design?*

There is quite a bit of work on design representation in
the sense of creating new forms [e.g., Peters and Tripp
(1976)] and, of course, most design methods are intimately
coupled with representation. A few explicit studies [e.g.,
Freeman (1978)] of design representation have been made and

there is an increasing amount of psychological research aimed
at some aspects of designing. Overall, however, there is very
little work being done explicitly on design representations.
As with design methods, eventually a firmer scientific basis
must be established.

Solution of Design Problems

A third area in which some underlying scientific theory
is needed to support our practical endeavors is the understanding of the logical or intellectual nature of design
problem-solving. People solve design problems all the time
even though we may not have a clear understanding of how it
is done, but people also fail at design problem-solving.

We can characterize the components of design solutions
and back up from this to derive the intellectual operations
necessary (e.g., establish a framework, generate alternatives,
select an appropriate one, etc.) necessary to arrive at an
acceptable design solution. (Obviously, the operations listed
above are at a very gross level of explanation.)

Some of the questions we would like answered are:

- *What are the intellectual operations (at a de-*
  tailed as well as macro-level) necessary to design?
- *Can we differentiate in terms of design operations*
  between varying design situations (such as design
  of a real-time control system and design of a data
  base)?
- *What are the larger phases of the design process*
  and are they the same for all types of problems?

Questions in this area are based on an informational view
of design -- that is, that design is an information-processing
activity and as such can be studied in information-processing
terms (i.e., informational objects and the operations on
them necessary to achieve new informational states).

There has been a good deal of work in other fields (and
some in computer science) on models of design in an attempt
to answer these questions   [see, for example, Freeman and
Newell (1971), and Bazjanac (1974)]. For the most part, this
work can be described as thought-provoking but not conclusive.

New research in this area should build on the earlier work
and make it specific to the area of software design. Software, while being purely symbolic, results in physical events
(outputs of the computer). Further, while it is a static
artifact, it represents and results in highly dynamic behavior.
These facts lead me to believe that such theoretical studies
of design have not been carried far enough yet in the field
of software.

Psychology of Design

It is also clear that we can learn from ·studying how
people actually design. There are two main subareas of in-
vestigation here:

- *cognitive psychology studies of people designing*
- *human factor studies of the languages, tools,*
  etc. used by designers

The first type of study typically results in a model of the
observed behavior that is consistent with already established
knowledge about cognitive behavior [see Levin (1976) for
example]. As our understanding of how people design is
deepened through such models, we will be able to augment more
intelligently what they can do.

Human factors are used here to describe studies ranging
from the impact of using linear versus graphical languages
to the effect of physical working environment to identifying
the factors of group dynamics. I have lumped together a number of investigations in which psychological studies or studies based on and consistent with psychology will result in
knowledge that guides us to a deeper understanding of design
and how to carry it out.

Design Structures

The final research area that I identify as potentially
contributing to software design I call design structures. The
other areas mentioned deal primarily with the design process;
this area deals with the artifacts being designed. Much of
computer science, of course, deals with the nature of software artifacts. An area that is not dealt with systematically,

however, is the study of the characteristics of classes of designs *qua* designs. Questions of interest center around properties of the designs and include:

- *What are the characterizing distinctions between designs?*
- *How can designs be cataloged and retrieved?*
- *Are there meaningful groups of design components that appear in different classes?*
- *Can necessary and sufficient sets of design structures be identified to build up entire classes of applications?*

Work that attempts to categorize all the algorithms of a particular type (e.g., sorting) is similar to what I have in mind here. However, the study of algorithms does not go far enough because it does not take into account the practical matters of actual designs. What I am referring to is more analogous to studies in biology or archeology that take existing organisms or artifacts and then classify and study them.

Long-Term Research

All of these topics introduced above will involve research of a long-term nature (even though some short-term results may ensue). Although, we might be able to use the results today, the objective is to establish a body of scientifically produced and verifiable knowledge about design on which a variety of undertakings can be based.

CURRENT DESIGN R AND D

Current work that falls in the design area is largely focused on program design (or on system design in a very general and abstract sense). When I look at the literature, I see papers concerned with several kinds of things:

Project experience: Typically, the theme is "We did the following in our project and this is what we think we observed." Such studies are useful, but obviously limited in what they can teach us.

Design representations: As noted above, current
work in this area is almost entirely devoted to
developing new representations. Experience with
them will give us some information, but such
experience is expensive to obtain and often in-
conclusive.

Design methods: In the past ten years many people
have realized that the methods followed in the
design of software can have a large impact on the
quality of the final product as well as on their
ability to control the design activity. This has
led to a proliferation of design methods. Such
methods are often either highly intuitive or very
formal, depending on the inclinations of their
inventors. Evaluating them runs into the same
problems noted with respect to design representations. Further, they tend to concentrate on detailed program design which increasingly is not
where the problems lie.

Tools: At present there appears to be an upsurge
of interest in tools for the design process. These
tools usually support a given method, or worse, are
not built consistent with any one coherent method.
Tools add several dimensions of complexity to the
task of augmenting or improving what designers do,
and I suspect that in many cases the efforts to
build design tools will fail when such efforts are
not based on a solid understanding of design.

Evaluation techniques: As noted above there is
some rudimentary work on evaluating designs along
different dimensions. Some of this work looks
promising but it is still in its early stages.

NEEDED DESIGN R AND D IN THE NEAR-TERM

In addition to the work already underway or that I have
suggested for the longer-term, there are several areas of
design research that should be more heavily emphasized in the

immediate future:

Method and tool evaluations: Comparison of existing
and proposed design methods and the tools to support
them is essential. We need to know their similarities
and differences; why some are successful and others
are not; what problems each is suitable for, and so
on. Almost all comparisons so far have been rudimentary at best; most are not based on a coherent view
of the design process.

Structures for specific designs: The idea of components is an old one in software but is largely
unexploited in production terms. The greatly de-
creased cost of memory and improvements in programming technology make the use of components more
feasible today than in the past. More work in this
area could have some good short-term payoffs.

Quality metrics: We have already noted the need for
measures of design quality. It is imperative that
such measures be used in practice on a widespread
scale so that experience with them can be obtained.

Design languages: Program design languages (PDL's)
have shown their usefulness in the practical arena
in a number of different situations. Improved
PDL's and additional representations at a higher
level of abstraction should be developed.

CONCLUDING REMARKS

A large amount of research is currently labelled software
engineering, but I believe that we must take a hard look at
just what it is producing. I recently reviewed the past four
years' volumes of the *IEEE Transactions on Software Engineering* to see if I could get some sense of what is currently
being done. Presumably work published in this journal is
primarily software engineering research by the current standards of the field. Allowing for some minor changes of wording, I found that the *Transactions* have used approximately 20
categories in which to place papers. Looking at these a

little more closely, I decided that these 20 categories could
be sorted into 7 types of research:

Abstract theories and techniques: Ideas are developed
primarily within some formal system. Examples are
abstract data types, program transformations, program
proving techniques, and design methods based on
Petri-nets. Included in this category is much of
"classical" computer science research.

Tools: Taken in a broad sense, this category includes languages, documentation forms, programs to
do specific tasks useful to the developer, and
entire systems to support software engineering.

Software structures: Work that results in general
building blocks and program or system forms includes
work on recovery blocks, capabilities, synchroniza-
tion primitives, virtual machines and some aspects
of data base work.

Empirical theory: Theories and generalizations are
developed from observations and/or are correlated
with observations. Included in this area is the
work on software science and program system dynamics.

Social and behavioral studies: Anything that
explicitly identifies and studies the human element in system development falls into this category.
Examples are studies of the social impacts of computing, psychology of programming, psychological
complexity of programs, and the psychological factors of user perceptions, displays, languages, and
so on.

Methodology: Research on the process of development belongs here. Included would be the science
of design work outlined above and the various papers
presenting new design methods.

Management: Any work related to management of system development is in this category. For example,
cost estimation, software engineering economics,
and productivity would be included.

The interesting thing to me was that a large fraction of the papers published fall into just the first category, with a few in the second and third groups. (Large amounts of work are done in the second and third areas, of course, and not reported in the *Transactions*.) The remainder of the categories had only token representation in the *Transactions*, and for the most part little work is reported on them in other places. Yet I believe strongly that good work in each of these other categories could contribute significantly to software engineering. In some instances, the contribution could be quite a bit larger than that of the work now being done in other areas. My conclusion is that work must be encouraged in these other areas.

I have two additional comments on the general subject of software engineering research. First, it is important to keep in mind that computer science and software engineering have different objectives that should not be confused. If they are confused, then both will suffer. Yet, this is not to say that they do not have significant areas of common concern. Computer science is concerned with the scientific study and description of algorithms, programs, the devices that interpret them, and the phenomena surrounding their creation and usage. Software engineering focuses on the application of this scientific knowledge to achieve stated technical, economic, and social goals.

Second, the term "software engineering" must be kept in perspective. In reality, we must be concerned with the "engineering of information systems" that contain as components hardware, software, people, and other artifacts. Because computer engineering, systems engineering, information systems development, and other disciplines have not addressed the software development question entirely successfully, it is useful to focus on software at this time in order to make progress. But, we must remember that software engineering exists only in a larger environment of entire systems, involving many different technical, economic, and social factors.

REFERENCES

Bazjanac, Vladimir (1974). Architectural design theory: Models of the design process, *In* "Basic Questions of Design Theory (W. R. Spillers, ed.), North-Holland/American Elsevier.

Boehm, B. W., et al (1973). "Characteristics of Software Quality," Tech. Report TRW-SS-73-09, TRW Systems Group, Redondo Beach, CA.

Freeman, Peter (1976). The central role of design in software engineering, *In* "Software Engineering Education," (A. I. Wasserman and P. Freeman, eds.), p. 116, Springer-Verlag.

Freeman, Peter (1978). Software design representation: analysis and improvements, *Software Practice and Experience 8*, 513-528.

Freeman, Peter, and Newell, Allen (1971). A model for functional reasoning in design, *Proc. 2nd Int'l. Joint Conf. on AI.*

Levin, Steven (1976). "Problem Selection in Computer Program Design," Ph.D. Thesis, University of California, Irvine, California.

McCabe, T. J. (1976). A complexity measure, *Trans. Sfw. Eng. SE-2(4),* 308.

Peters, L. J., and Tripp, L. L. (1976). Software design representation schemes, *In* "Computer Software Engineering," (J. Fox, ed.), p. 31, Polytechnic Press, Division of John Wiley.

Simon, H. A. (1969). "Sciences of the Artificial," MIT Press.

Yourdon, E., and Constantine, L. L. (1979). "Structured Design," Prentice-Hall.

EVOLUTIONARY PROGRAMMING

Carl Hewitt

Massachusetts Institute of Technology
Cambridge, Massachusetts

EVOLUTION

The documentation, implementations (we use the plural because we want to allow for multiple implementations), and
runtime environment of useful software systems evolve asyn-
chronously and continually. This is particularly true of
large systems for applications such as reservations, programming environments, real-time control, data base query and update, and document preparation. Implementations change because of the development of new hardware and algorithms. Documentation (including tutoring programs such as [Burton and
Brown (1976); Goldstein (1976); Genesereth (1979); and Miller
(1979)]) changes to keep up with other changes. Runtime environments change because of changes in legislation and other
unforeseen events rearrange the physical environment.
Neither fully automatic program synthesis nor fully automatic program proving have been very successful thus far in
dealing with large software systems. We believe that it is
necessary to build environments to interact with software
engineers in the course of the *co-evolution* of the partial
interface specifications and implementations of a system.
Realistic software systems impose the requirement that the
interface specifications of modules must be allowed to evolve
along with the implementations. This situation makes it correspondingly more difficult to construct a fully automatic
programmer for such systems. In case of inconsistency between
the partial interface specifications, runtime environment, and
implementation of a large system, it may be desirable to

modify *any* of them. It is naive to believe that complete interface specifications can be laid down once and for all time
in a large software system and the implementations of the
modules derived by top-down stepwise refinement.

It is important to realize that the *co-evolution* of implementations and interface specifications is an entirely natural
and fruitful process. In most applications it is fruitless to
delay implementation until complete and final interface specifications have been provided.

The history of the development of text editors on interactive systems provides a good illustration of the co-evolution of implementations and interface specifications. In the
late fifties when text editors were first being developed, it
would have been completely impossible to have developed interface specifications or implementations for current generation
text editors. It was necessary for users and implementors of
text editors to evolve the systems over a long time period in
the context of an evolving hardware base in order to reach the
current state of development. Furthermore, it seems rather
clear that interactive text editors will continue to evolve at
a rapid pace for quite some time in the future.

Exploration of what it is possible to implement provides
guidance on what are reasonable partial interface specifications. As experience accumulates in using an implementation,
more of the real needs and possible benefits are discovered
causing the partial interface specifications to change. An
important consideration in a proposed change is the difficulty
of modifying the implementation and documentation. Conversely,
implementors attempt to create systems that have the generality
to cope with anticipated directions of evolution. Partial interface specifications in large systems change gradually over
a long period of time through a process of negotiation.

THE DESCRIPTION SYSTEM OMEGA

One fundamental tool in our approach is the description
system Omega which can be used to describe properties of objects. It is intended to facilitate use of the following
kinds of descriptions:

PARTIAL descriptions are used to express whatever properties of system. Descriptions of realistic systems such as air traffic control involve
inevitable simplifications and approximations.
It is useless to wait for a complete description
of an air traffic control system because the goal
of complete description is unattainable.

INCREMENTAL descriptions which enable us to
further describe objects when more information
becomes available and are a necessary feature for
the effective use of *partial descriptions*. For
example at some point as the velocity of jet airplanes increases it will be necessary to take the
Coriolis effect into account in the air traffic
control system.

MULTIPLE descriptions which enable us to
ascribe multiple overlapping descriptions to an
object which is used for multiple purposes. Multiple descriptions are important in multiple
specifications and proofs because different properties of an object might be useful in different
contexts.

Our description system is used in stating partial specifications of programs, as a powerful flexible notation to
state type declarations, and as a notation to express conditions that are tested during program execution. The assumptions and constraints on the objects manipulated by a program
are an integral part of the program and can be used both as
checks when the program is running and as useful information
which can be exploited by other systems which examine the program, such as translators, optimizers, indexers, etc. We believe that bugs occurring in programs are frequently caused
by the violation of implicit assumptions about the environment
in which the program is intended to operate. Therefore many
advantages can be drawn by a language that encourages the
programmer to state such assumptions explicitly and by a system which is able to detect when they are violated.

A PROGRAMMERS' APPRENTICE

A group at M.I.T. is engaged in a long term research effort to build an interactive system (called the *Programmers'
Apprentice*) to aid in the construction and evolution of large
software systems using partial, multiple, incremental interfaces between users and implementors of software systems. The
Programmers' Apprentice effort [Rich, Shrobe, Waters, Sussman,
and Hewitt (1978); Shrobe (1978); Waters (1978); Hewitt (1978);
and Rich, Shrobe, and Waters (1979)] builds on antecedent and
similar work by Floyd (1971); Hewitt (1971); Sussman (1975);
Hewitt and Smith (1975); Rich and Shrobe (1976); Yonezawa
(1977); and Moriconi (1978).

Figure 1 shows the relationship between the users of a
module M, its partial multiple interface specifications, its
implementations, and the knowledge of the runtime environment
of M.

The contractual external interface of a module M should
be as close as possible to an absolute interface in the sense
that any external module which uses M should only rely on
properties of M implied by its external interface and the contractual knowledge of the runtime environment for M. Notice
that associated with each implementation of M, we have versions of the interface specification and knowledge of the runtime environment that are private to each implementation. The
private versions contain the documentation that is special to
each one.

The contractual knowledge of runtime environment is the
shared knowledge relied on by both the users and implementors
of M. Examples are the laws of physics in a bubble chamber
analysis program, the tax law for an income tax preparation
program, and the number of physical tracks on a disk for a
memory management module.

A primary goal of the *Programmers' Apprentice* is to make
explicit how each module depends on the partial interface specifications of other modules and the knowledge of the runtime
environment, how each implementation of a module meets its
partial interface specifications, and how each implementation
depends on the knowledge of the runtime environment. The

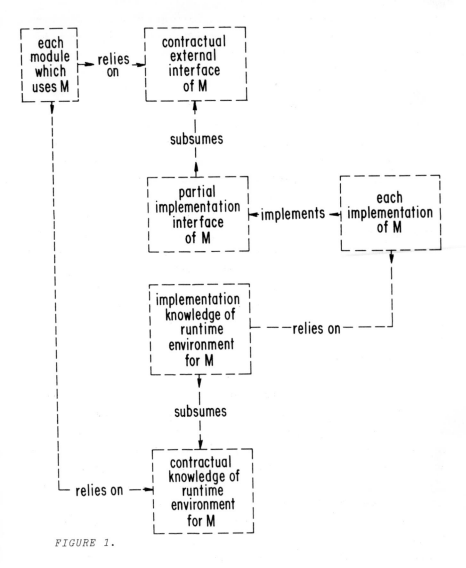

FIGURE 1.

proposed *Programmers' Apprentice* will gradually make the above
dependencies explicit through a process of *symbolic evaluation*
[Deutsch (1973); Hewitt and Smith (1975); Yonezawa (1977);
King (1976); Clarke (1976); Shrobe (1978); Hewitt (1978);
Shrobe (1978); and Cheatham, Holloway, and Townley (1978)].
Symbolic evaluation consists of executing the implementation
of a module M on abstract input using the partial interface

specifications of modules it uses. An important purpose of
symbolic evaluation is to make explicit exactly how the partial interface specifications of M are satisfied. Symbolic
evaluation ensures that a module M only depends on the partial
interface specifications and the knowledge of the runtime
environment of the modules which it uses and does not depend
on idiosyncratic properties of particular implementations. It
establishes and maintains an interface between users and
implementors of a module. An explicit record of dependencies
is necessary for the successful creation and co-evolution of
the documentation, implementations, and knowledge of runtime
environment of a large software system.

    Evolving systems of the kind we are describing will re-
quire the capabilities of expert programmers for a long time
into the future. Our proposed *Programmers' Apprentice* plays
mainly an advisory and bookkeeping role. We believe that this
state of affairs is entirely appropriate given the current
state of the art in fully automatic program synthesis and
program proving.

CONCRETE PROGRAMMING

    Program development is traditionally performed in several
separate stages: program editing, compilation, and testing.
Most programming systems require that a complete program be
present before testing can begin. Every time a move is made,
for instance writing a procedure invocation, the programmer
must *imagine* what its effect will be on typical data the program will encounter. In this way it is very easy to lose
track of the intermediate states during the execution of a
program. Bugs that are introduced because the intermediate
states do not conform to user expectations will remain un-
noticed for a long time.

    By contrast, we are building a new system called Tinker
for program development based on a methodology which we call
concrete programming. An important design goal is for Tinker
to support program construction, abstraction, and testing as
a single unified process.

In Tinker programming tasks will be integrated and generalized into the creation of successive *snapshots*. A snapshot
represents a single step in the evolution of a program. Code
for parts of the program may be only partially complete at
each step. The snapshot shows the current progress of the
computation on a concrete example. Every step will produce a
new partial description of the program that will be integrated
with previous descriptions; this activity leads to the construction of a more complete program.

The user supplies examples, test cases, and information
about the environment in which the program will run. When the
user specifies an operation in the course of working out a
concrete example, it will be performed on the example, and the
user can see immediately if the results are as expected. This
immediate feedback allows a user to correct a faulty expression on the spot, instead of burying it deep inside a larger
program where it is harder to diagnose it as the source of
the error.

Tinker remembers all the examples given to it, even after
the definition is complete. If the program is later extended,
the old examples can be run again to make sure that they still
work.

Thus Tinker encourages concrete program development. Program writing and program testing, which usually occur in separate stages, will take place as one unified process in Tinker.

The user and system interact by means of a high-resolution
display, allowing large amounts of information to be made
available at once. The graphical user interface is based on
the use of menus and pointing devices.

Our goal is to implement a system which can be used in
practical applications. It should not be limited in the size
or class of programs for which it can be used. The greatest
freedom will be left to the user: editing, tracing, and
testing can be performed in any order. Examples, declarations,
and commentary are optional and can be introduced at any point
in the development of the program.

Users may change their minds often, modifying or deleting
at unpredictable times parts of the program or structures
being constructed.

We propose to use the description system Omega to *partially* describe data and programs. Rather than being completely unspecified, or as specific as a concrete example, a structure may be partially specified by using descriptions. Every instance of that structure should satisfy those descriptions. These descriptions can include information that would appear in traditional type declarations, saying that an object is a number or a list. They can also include more complex assertions about the object such as constraints on parts of the object or its relation to other objects. Tinker will use these descriptions to check whether an operation can be legally performed on a symbolic object and to perform type checking. When the system knows the type of an object, it will display a menu of operations the abstract data type supports for the user to choose from.

Descriptions will be particularly useful in performing symbolic execution of the program. At the same time operations are performed on examples, Tinker will perform symbolic execution on the descriptions of those examples. In this way, it will have information about accessible data at any point in the program. This information can be used to determine the allowed operations on the data and to check the correctness of the use of procedures with respect to precisely stated preconditions.

The description system also will be used to furnish the user with information about any particular object. For instance, it will present a description of the object, it will tell which operation created the object, and it will indicate dependencies with other objects.

We have been actively involved in the development of concurrent systems [Hewitt, Attardi, and Lieberman (1979)]. One of our goals is to apply the techniques of concrete programming to this area. We need to aid the user in visualizing the relationships that occur in concurrent systems. One possibility is the further extension of the *event diagrams* of Hewitt (1976).

ANIMATION

A number of techniques have been adopted for fully
exploiting the capabilities of the high-resolution display as
a flexible user interface with a high rate of exchange of information.

Among these, of course, are windows and menus for structuring information [Engelbart (1970); EMACS (1977); Swinehart
(1974); Buneman, Morgan, and Zisman (1977); Ingalls (1978);
Teitelman (1977); and CADR (1978)], highlights reverse video,
and flashing for focusing attention, icons and pointers to
represent common structures and visualize sharing, and animation to convey the progress of a computation.

Also, we have been involved in the implementation of multiple windows and menu-driven operations on CADR. In addition,
we have worked on the implementation of Actl, a new actor-
based programming language, on CADR. And we have worked on
animation and implemented in particular a system, called Di-
agrammer, that is able to arrange on the display diagrams,
made with boxes and arrows, using knowledge-based heuristics.

Tinker will both *record* and *playback* programs. Using
Tinker to playback a program will step through its execution.
The user will playback the program at varying levels of detail, suppressing unwanted details. If a bug is encountered,
the user can examine the execution of the program at varying
levels of detail until the bug is located. When *recording,*
operations will be checked for validity, and remembered as
part of a program. Programs will be edited by playing back
the program and making changes to the definition. We shall
provide facilities for examining data structures at varying
levels of detail.

Test cases will be presented using pictures on the screen
representing program variables and procedure arguments. If
the value of a variable is used in a program, the corresponding operation is performed on the example and shown immediately on the screen. The user will do the computation on a
specific test case, and the system will remember the sequence
of operations performed to construct the program. As much as
possible, the user will communicate with the computer by

selecting items from a menu rather than by typing. Tinker will present the user with choice among a small number of operations, and the user will pick one by using a pointing device. Typing will be necessary only when introducing symbolic names. The menu serves as a continual reminder of the available operations and the user will not need to look them up in a manual.

We are experimenting with a new technique for introducing conditionals in programs. Typically, a thorough test of a program requires that every path of the program be exercised by the examples. Henry Lieberman has implemented the ability that the user can present the system with a particular test case and develop code which deals with the case illustrated by that example. The user may then present Tinker with a different test case. When the second reaches a point where the computation differs from the first case, Tinker will construct a conditional. The user will then be asked what predicate should be used to distinguish the two cases.

HISTORICAL NOTE

The late fifties saw the initiation of a programming methodology which attempted to abstract programs from examples of *input-output behavior*. It consists in the use of a system which attempts to *automatically* infer what operations to be performed from a mere presentation of a set of examples. Such a system might be asked to synthesize a *PRIME* program from the knowledge that (*PRIME 2*) is 2, (*PRIME 3*) is 3, (*PRIME 4*) is 5, and (*PRIME 5*) is 7. Although people can infer procedures from examples in simple cases, in general this is a much harder problem, and we believe it is currently beyond the state of the art for realistic programming situations. Tinker will require that all operations to be done be explicitly or implicitly invoked by the user.

Some early ideas on abstracting procedures from example computations were described in Hewitt (1971). The abstraction mechanism used in the current implementation of Tinker uses some of these ideas. However this early work suffered from the critical limitation that it did not make use of a display interface with a pointing device to track the *flow* of the computation.

Tinker is already further developed in certain directions and more incremental than these systems. For example previous systems did not permit conditionals to be integrated into the code being developed after some examples had been presented. Also concrete programming differs from and goes beyond programming by example in several respects mentioned earlier.

One of the best early attempts to construct a system for programming by abstracting from example executions was David Canfield Smith's *Pygmalion* system. Pygmalion was written in an early version of the SmallTalk language, which shares the object-oriented message passing philosophy of actors derived in large part from SIMULA. It combined a methodology of programming by menu selection with definition of programs by abstraction from examples allowing programs to be executed before being completely specified.

Pygmalion was also trying to develop a *graphical programming language*, a language which allowed a user to program entirely in terms of pictures. The representation of a program was an animated movie. Internally, the program was compiled into a *machine language* which operated on graphical objects. This machine language then had to be interpreted when the program was run.

CONCLUSIONS

This paper has dealt with tools being developed to facilitate the evolution of software systems. The description system Omega and the knowledge embedding system Ether are being developed to describe the knowledge bases involved. The *Programmers' Apprentice* project is working to expand our ability to uncover and express the interdependencies between the code and documentation of these systems. Concrete programming in systems like Tinker is developing tools for evolving implementations on the basis of new test cases. Animation provides means to effectively display changes in evolving systems.

While we feel a graphical programming language is a worth-
while area for research, we want to decouple graphical representation of programs from the ideas of programming by example
and menu selection. We plan to integrate these new ideas with
the more traditional textual representations of programs.
Representations of programs as text have advantages for some
purposes. A textual representation is much more compact than
a graphical representation allowing modules of a realistic
size to be displayed.

We are also building on the work of Curry on developing
programs from abstract examples. We intend to make use of
our description system to bridge the continuum from the completely abstract examples of Curry to the completely concrete
examples of Pygmalion and Biermann and Ramachandran.

ACKNOWLEDGMENTS

Preliminary versions of Actl (by Henry Lieberman), the
Apiary (by Jeff Schiller), Director (by Ken Kahn), Ether (by
Bill Kornfeld), Forpas (by Dick Waters), Omega (by Giuseppe
Attardi and Maria Simi), Reason (by Howie Shrobe), Tinker (by
Henry Lieberman), and XPRT (by Luc Steels) have been imple-
mented on the M.I.T. CADR system.

The development of the ideas expressed in this paper has
been the work of a large group of people over many years. The
intellectual roots go back to the early emphasis by Minsky and
Papert of the importance of "debugging" in problem solving
(especially programming). We are indebted to our colleagues
Gerry Sussman and Pat Winston for many an inspiring discussion
on how to best incorporate these ideas in practical systems.
In turn we are indebted to thesis students and staff members
Beppe Attardi, Jerry Barber, Will Clinger, Ken Kahn, Henry
Lieberman, Chuck Rich, Jeff Schiller, Howie Shrobe, Maria
Simi, Luc Steels, Dick Waters, and Aki Yonezawa for providing
the hard work and ideas necessary to make this area into more
of a sicence.

Tinker builds on work by Bauer, Curry, Biermann and
Ramachandran, and Smith on programming by example. Dave Smith
and Gale Curry were particularly helpful to us in providing
demonstrations of their systems.

BIBLIOGRAPHY

Bauer, M. A. (1975). A basis for the acquisition of Procedures from Protocols, *Proc. 4th Int'l. Joint Conf. Artif.
Intell.*, 226-231.

Biermann, A. W., and Ramachandran, K. (1976). Constructing
programs from example computations, *IEEE Transactions
on Software Engineering SE-2(3)*.

Buneman, O., Morgan, H., and Zisman, M. (1977). Display
facilities for decision support, *DATA BASE Winter Issue*.

Burton, R., and Brown, J. S. (1976). A tutoring and student
modeling paradigm for gaming environments, *SIGCSE Bulletin
8(1)*, 236-246.

Cheatham, T. E., Holloway, G. H., and Townley, J. A. (1978).
"Symbolic Evaluation and the Analysis of Programs," TR-19-
78, Aiken Computation Laboratory, Harvard University.

Clarke, L. (1976). A system to generate test data and sym-
bolically execute programs, *IEEE TSE-2(3)*, 215-222.

Curry, G. J. (1978). "Programming by Abstract Demonstration,"
Technical Report No. 78-03-02, Dept. of Computer Science,
University of Washington.

Dahl, O. J., and Nygaard, K. (1968). Class and subclass
declarations, *In* "Simulation Programming Languages," (J.
N. Buxton, ed.), North-Holland, 158-174.

DeJong, S. P., and Zloof, M. (1978). System for business
automation: Programming language, *Comm. ACM 21(5)*.

Deutsch, P. (1973). "An Interactive Program Verifier," Report
No. CSL-73-1, Xerox PARC, Palo Alto, California.

Engelbart, D. C. (1970). "Advanced Intellect-Augmentation
Techniques," Final Report, SRI International, Menlo Park,
California.

Genesereth, M. R. (1979). The role of plans in automated con-
sultation, *Proc. 6th Int'l. Joint Conf. Artif. Intell.*,
Tokyo, Japan.

Goldstein, Ira P. (1976). "The Computer as Coach: An
Athletic Paradigm for Intellectual Education," AI Memo
389, Artificial Intelligence Laboratory, M.I.T., Cambridge,
Massachusetts.

Hewitt, C. (1972). "Procedural Semantics: Models of Procedures and Teaching of Procedures," *In* Natural Language Processing, (Randall Rustin, ed.), Algorithmics.

Hewitt, C. (1977). Viewing control structures as patterns of passing messages, *A. I. Journal 8(3)*, 323-364.

Hewitt, C., and Smith, B. (1975). Towards a programming apprentice, *IEEE Transactions on Software Engineering SE-1(1)*, 26-45.

Hewitt, C., Attardi, G., and Lieberman, H. (1979). Specifying and proving properties of guardians for distributed systems, *Proc. International Symposium on the Semantics of Concurrent Computation*, Evian-les-bains, France.

Hewitt, C., Attardi, G., and Lieberman, H. (1979). "Security and Modularity in Message Passing," First International Conference on Distributed Systems, Huntsville, Alabama.

Ingalls, D. H. H. (1978). "The Smalltalk-76 Programming System Design and Implementation," Conference Record of the Fifth Annual ACM Symposium on Principles of Programming Languages, Tucson, Arizona, 9-16.

Kahn, K. M. (1978). "DIRECTOR Guide," AI Memo 482, Artificial Intelligence Laboratory, M.I.T., Cambridge, Massachusetts.

King, J. C. (1974). "A New Approach to Program Testing," IBM Research Report RC-5037.

Kornfeld, W. A. (1979). Using parallel processing for problem solving, *Proc. 6th Int'l. Joint Conf. on Artif. Intell.*, Tokyo, Japan.

Miller, M. L. (1979). "Planning and Debugging in Elementary Programming," Unpublished Doctoral Dissertation, M.I.T., Cambridge, Massachusetts.

Moriconi, Mark S. (1978). "A Designer/Verifier's Assistant," Technical Report CSL-80, SRI International, Menlo Park, California.

Rich, C., and Shrobe, H. (1976). Initial report on a LISP programmer's apprentice, AI-TR-354, *IEEE Transactions on Software Engineering SE-4(6)*, November 1978, 456-467.

Rich, C., Shrobe, H. E., Waters, R. C., Sussman, G. J., and Hewitt, C. E. (1978). "Programming Viewed as an Engineering Activity," A.I. Memo 459, Artificial Intelligence Laboratory, M.I.T., Cambridge, Massachusetts.

Rich, C., Shrobe, H. E., and Waters, R. C. (1979). "Computer
    Aided Evolutionary Design for Software Engineering," A.I.
    Memo 506, Artificial Intelligence Laboratory, M.I.T.,
    Cambridge, Massachusetts.

Shrobe, H. (1978). "Logic and Reasoning for Complex Program
    Understanding," Ph.D. Thesis, M.I.T., Cambridge, Massa-
    chusetts.

Simon, H. (1963). "The Heuristic Compiler," Memorandum RM-
    3588-PR, The Rand Corporation, Santa Monica, California.

Smith, D. C. (1975). "PYGMALION: A Creative Programming
    Environment," AIM-260, Artificial Intelligence Laboratory,
    Stanford University, Stanford, California.

Sussman, G. J. (1975). "A Computer Model of Skill Acquisi-
    tion," American Elsevier.

Waters, R. C. (1978). "Automatic Analysis of the Logical
    Structure of Programs," TR-492, Artificial Intelligence
    Laboratory, M.I.T., Cambridge, Massachusetts.

Wulf, W. A. (1976). "Abstraction and Verification in ALPHARD:
    Introduction to Language and Methodology," ISI/RR-76-46.

Yonezawa, A. (1977). "Specification and Verification Tech-
    niques for Parallel Programs Based on Message Passing
    Semantics," LCS/TR-191, M.I.T., Cambridge, Massachusetts.

REMOVING THE LIMITATIONS OF
NATURAL LANGUAGE
(WITH PRINCIPLES BEHIND
THE RSA LANGUAGE)

Douglas T. Ross

SofTech, Inc.
Waltham, MA

INTRODUCTION

In a field as fast moving as ours, ten years into the
future is a long time. Therefore when I received an invita-
tion to participate in this workshop, presenting a topic of
my own choosing which I thought could make an important contribution to research over the next ten years, that seemed
like quite a challenge. I did not want to come up with a dry
hole that would be exhausted with eight years still to run.
I wanted a topic with an objective that could be understood
now, but which in all probability still would be just as stimulating and challenging ten years from now. I think my topic
satisfies those criteria. My uncertainty concerns only my
ability to make the topic and the objective understandable
now, for I am certain that if I can accomplish that, their
viability ten years hence will be unquestioned.

The topic is most concisely stated in terms of my objective:

Objective: To be able to use any and all
natural language in such a way as
to rigorously permit perfect understanding of the intended meaning.

On the surface, this may seem to some to be absurd and un-
achievable. Such a natural reaction is the primary foundation

for my confidence that the topic will remain viable ten years
hence. Realizing that I am indeed serious in my proposal,
however, the next reaction which is most natural is to become
analytically critical of my formulation. Every word used is
very ordinary, but if the sentence is to have anything other
than the gut reaction absurd meaning, then I must intend
almost every word in the sentence to be interpreted with some
particular technical meaning. This is indeed true, and in the
following paragraphs, I will attempt to convey those particular meanings. In the Appendix, I reproduce the slides used
in my oral presentation at the workshop, to illustrate my own
approach which shows promise of meeting the objective and
which also serves to illustrate the technical concepts involved.

OUR DEPENDENCE ON NATURAL LANGUAGE

    I hope that the importance of the topic (assuming I can
establish its viability) also will be unquestioned. Quite
simply stated -- in my view it is an inescapable fact that
every possible problem and every possible solution in any
conceivable subject ultimately must hinge upon natural language used by humans. In fact, in my view, nature has no
problems, it merely runs on and on. Only human understanding
of observed phenomena -- understanding expressible only in
language considered natural by the possessor of that understanding -- allows an undesired state of affairs to be formulated as a problem, much less to be solved. Even technical
languages, artificial languages, mathematics, and logic require interpretation as natural language to be meaningful,
much less useful. Therefore, all language ultimately becomes
natural language in use, and even though some nonlinguistic
gestalt may yield the first insight of understanding, all
rational subsequent thought takes place, even within a single
mind, by means of natural (visual or verbal) language.
    Therefore, I claim that our ultimate dependence on natural
language, as I intend that term to be interpreted, is absolutely and fundamentally inescapable. Given such dependence,
and given the supreme challenges of modern-day undertakings

of all sorts, I believe that attempting to achieve the above-
stated objective by its very nature is inherently of the ut-
most importance. Even small progress will increase our critical faculties. Significant progress will have the potential
of far reaching consequence in all fields of endeavor.

CONTROLLING IMPRECISION AND AMBIGUITY

So let us begin with the dismemberment of my Objective
statement, elaborating each key phrase or word into my intended technical meaning. The preceding paragraph shows that
I intend the phrase "any and all natural language" to include
artificial languages as well as languages in any written form,
including graphical. In use, all such languages are "natural"
in my view. The most obvious problem with natural language
for technical purposes is that it is notoriously imprecise and
ambiguous. I looked up the word "run" in a large dictionary
once, and counted 151 distinct meanings listed! Although this
may be an extreme case, most words are highly context dependent. To overcome this imprecision and ambiguity, the key
phrase is "be able to use ... in such a way ..." In other
words the key step must lie in establishing a "way" in which
natural language is to be used so that both imprecision and
ambiguity can be overcome. Sufficient detail is to overcome
imprecision, and sufficient context is to overcome ambiguity.
My own means to accomplish this end I call *RSA*, standing
for Ross's Structured Analysis. (My originally-coined name
"Structured Analysis" was usurped into the public domain without adopting my meaning.) RSA uses a graphical diagramming
language in which boxes and arrows provide a framework into
which natural language expressions are embedded. The box-and-
arrow framework obeys rigorous syntax and semantics rules, but
the language itself is neutral or content-free, in the same
way that punctuation marks, gestures, and voice emphasis have
no independent meaning. Just as punctuation takes priority
over and dominates the semantics of words being punctuated,
the graphical semantic constraints of RSA force the natural
language expression semantics to be understood only in certain
ways. This idea of forcing the interpretation of natural

language expressions to conform to structure rigorously
imposed by the graphic aspects of the written RSA language is
the underlying mechanism which makes the entire enterprise
feasible.

The "such a way" of RSA depends strongly on the prior
establishment of a disciplined and highly structured way of
thinking, which is applied before thoughts are expressed in
the natural-graphic language. In fact, RSA is primarily a
structured-thought discipline, with a graphic means of expression. The discipline imposed does not limit in any way the
subject matter being thought about, but, again like the universal, content-free punctuation, enforces orderly rules of
concept formation and exposition. Certain poetic use of
language may be beyond its scope, but for technical matters,
the rules and discipline can be taught and learned so that
they apply independent of subject. Once a certain skill level
is achieved through practice, the thought discipline seems to
be very natural and uninhibiting, and in fact becomes the
preferred mode of thinking for most practitioners.

Continuing with the analysis of the wording of the objective, the phrase "rigorously permit" requires that a few
words be said about how RSA actually works. *RSA diagrams*
consist of standard 8½ x 11 inch sheets containing boxes,
arrows, and a few other notations, in addition to the natural
language expressions which name the boxes and label the arrows.
Following the thought discipline of RSA, an *RSA model* of a
chosen subject is created as an interconnected set of RSA
diagrams. The following definition of the word "model" is
adopted.

> *Definition:* M is a *model* of S if M can be used
>   to answer questions about S.

where S is some body of subject matter. In an RSA model,
each box on a diagram represents some detail of a part of the
subject expressed by the whole diagram, and itself may be
further detailed by box-and-arrow structure on another diagram. The top-most box of a model represents the entire
subject as a single box, which is in this fashion successively
detailed in a top-down hierarchic decomposition. No diagram
can contain more than six boxes, and the arrows which create

the boundary of a box rigorously carry through to the boundary of the corresponding detail diagram, so that a fully interconnected box-and-arrow structure results. Each box and each arrow at each level is suitably labeled with language expressions natural to be subject matter, and because there are rigorous rules of interpretation of the arrow structure as it threads its way through the box and diagram structure, semantic rules of interpretation are enforced upon the meaning of all of the natural language expressions. The effect is to supply greater and greater precision by decomposing to greater and greater levels of detail while at the same time the constraints of the arrow structure force more and more of the possible ambiguous meanings to be discarded as not fitting -- leaving as the only possible meaning the one that the author of the model intended.

OVERCOMING FUNDAMENTAL LIMITATIONS

This all would be well and good if things worked out just this simply, but they don't. As the Appendix shows in more detail, there are fundamental limitations on the degree to which this very rational machinery can be pressed. It is these limitations and the steps taken to overcome them that constitute the long-term research challenge. The direction to go (for RSA at least) is quite clear and philosophically satisfying, but the proof of the pudding will require a great deal more experience and illustration than has been acquired thus far.

Both the limitations and the steps to overcome them are outlined in the Appendix. In brief, it turns out that every RSA model has an *orientation* consisting of context, viewpoint, and purpose, which, in a fundamental way, bound and limit the amount of the subject that can be exposed from that chosen orientation, and determine its structure, as well. No single model can cover its subject completely. In fact, a more practical definition of "model" is as follows:

Definition: M is a *model* of S if M can be used
to answer (a well defined set of)
questions about S (to a tolerance
adequate for a stated purpose).

In other words, a single model is inherently limited in both
scope and precision. In fact, a single model may itself lack
the structural strength to rule out all ambiguity. In any
case, multiple models are required.

In RSA there are a limited number of rigorously defined
junctors for joining multiple models into *networks of models*
and for relating their subject matters syntactically and se-
mantically. This added machinery, in theory (and this is what
must be investigated by extensive further research) will overcome the limitations inherent in single models to allow my
stated Objective to be achieved. The RSA approach is outlined in the Appendix, but in brief, the argument is as
follows:

The hierarchic decomposition of every RSA model is bounded
by an inner and an outer boundary. The *outer boundary* is the
boundary of the top-level box. The *inner boundary* is the collection of the boundaries of all of the finest-level detail
boxes. The arrow structure of the model is a network of connections between the outer and the inner boundary boxes (all
of the boxes of the intermediate diagrams are purely imaginary
representations of the structured thought process of the analysis expressed in the model). They represent the intended
parse of the model structure enforcing the intended interpretation.

The RSA Fundamental Limitation of Viewpoint states that
there is an *atomic level* for every model beyond which further
detailing from that viewpoint is not possible. In order to
penetrate to further detail, new orientations and hence different models must be brought into play. This is indeed
possible, and appropriate additional orientations do indeed
allow penetration to the subatomic level (with respect to the
original orientation) until the fundamental limitation again
forces a halt. But again, further orientations and models can
be invoked to continue still further. In this way, the limitation of detailing of the original model can be overcome as

is possible, because the entire collection of models forms an
integrated network and it is the entire structure of the network of models that works to overcome both the imprecision
and the ambiguity of the natural language expressions occurring throughout the models.

The above description indicates how the limitation for the
inner boundary may be overcome, but again, there is another
fundamental limitation which stops this endeavor from reaching
arbitrary perfection. The culprit in this case is the outer
boundary, for ultimately the understanding of every natural
language expression in the downward-extending network of
models depends upon the context provided by the originating
boundary for interpretation. The outer boundary itself consists of labeled arrows interconnecting the entire network of
models into the outermost context. The labels on these
arrows, dangling loose, impose a further fundamental limitation of imprecision and ambiguity which still must be overcome.

Fortunately in RSA the machinery appears to be available,
and is outlined in the Appendix. The argument may be outlined
as follows:

Every RSA model in theory consists of two dual decompositions each using the same box-and-arrow notation. The most
common dual choice is *things* versus *happenings*, expressed by
noun phrases and verb phrases in the natural language. In an
activity decomposition, boxes represent activities or happenings and arrows represent data or things. In the *data decomposition*, the opposite is true, so that boxes represent
data and arrows represent activities. Both decompositions
(which have quite independent structures) are cross related by
the RSA "tie" process which links the two decompositions together into a single model corresponding to the chosen orientation.

The outer boundary of a model is represented by the
structure of external arrows. Although few in number, these
arrows actually represent (for an activity model) data which
is just as finely subdivided as the atomic level of the boxes
of the orientation. (In colloquial terms, each arrow has a
cross section that corresponds to a highly-structured cable

of cables, with many fine wires transmitting fine-level pieces
of data.) In order to pin down (in activity terms) the precise nature of these data details, two stages of dual RSA decomposition yield an activity context which surrounds the
"top" of the original model, providing the outside interface
to its outer boundary. In other words, switching to the dual
data domain, sufficient data decomposition modeling is performed to arrive at an appropriate atomic level of data detailing (perhaps involving a network with several orientations
as before in order to penetrate adequately into the subatomic
data levels). This constellation of (by now) well-defined
data then is analyzed in activity terms to provide a description of the ultimate sources and nature of the original outer
boundary arrows, in all detail. Again, a sufficient amount of
such modeling can, in theory, overcome to any desired degree
the imprecision and ambiguity of the outer boundary. Therefore, the argument is complete in that sufficient modeling in
both directions can overcome the fundamental limitations of
both the inner and outer boundaries of the original model to
any desired degree.

PERFECT UNDERSTANDING

Returning to the original Objective, the expression "to
rigorously permit perfect understanding of the intended meaning" by now should be clear. There are definite rules for
the proper reading and understanding of individual RSA models
as well as networks of models. If the author of such a network of models has properly used the structuring machinery,
so that (to the required tolerance) only his intended meaning
passes through the sieve of that structure, then any reader
trained in the rigorous rules of interpretation must arrive
at the same meaning -- if he is able to understand the network
of models at all.

The word "permit" itself has a very particular meaning in
terms of RSA. According to the theory behind RSA, the process
described here can make models understandable, but there is no
way that the author can force understanding into the mind of a
reader. The word "permit" means that any individual who

becomes a fully trained and practicing reader of RSA -- which
includes learning how to obey the rules before anything else
-- will know whether he understands the meaning of the network
or not. If after following the rules of readership, that
reader simply "can't get his mind around the subject", he will
know that, and he will assert that he does *not* understand the
model. On the other hand, whenever that trained reader asserts
that he does understand -- then his understanding will be as
perfect as the author has expressed. Whatever the tolerance
of authorship (in terms of residual imprecision and ambiguity),
the author will be understood to that degree of perfection.

In order for this concept itself (i.e., my originally
stated Objective) to be fully understood is, I am sure, at
least a ten year research challenge. I hope however that this
brief dissertation has at least been understandable enough to
engender some enthusiastic participation by those who might be
able to contribute either to the research itself or to the
exercise and exploitation of these concepts in important
practical applications.

POSTSCRIPT

RSA derives from, and is in fact an integral part of *Plex*,
a natural philosophy on which all of my research since the
late 1950's has been based. In the form of SofTech's trade-
marked Structured Analysis and Design Technique (SADT™), the
basic principles and notations have been taught to hundreds of
people of various backgrounds since 1974, and SADT has been
successfully used in a wide range of projects from very technical subjects (telephonic switching system design, financial
management system design) to very high levels (requirements
definition for military and industrial systems, long range
planning, project design and control). The largest single
application (since 1973) is the industry-wide Air Force ICAM
Program for Integrated Computer Aided Manufacturing. Most of
the features of SADT activity modeling are incorporated in the
ICAM Definition Methodology, $IDEF_0$, used by all ICAM

SADT ⓣ *is a trademark of SofTech, Inc.*

contractors for the modeling of all aspects of manufacturing and for integration into the overall ICAM Architecture of Manufacturing.

In my view, RSA in its various forms is merely the first systematized methodology of thinking which allows the formal treatment of natural language in technologically useful ways. I believe that once it becomes more widely recognized that solid, rigorous science can indeed be carried out in this seemingly intractable and nebulous area, other researchers may formulate similar but different approaches to achieve the Objective which forms the theme of this paper, just as at one time there were several schools of thought actively contributing to the development of quantum mechanics in physics. I hope that within the ten year span, my original and preferred term "structured analysis" can reenter the common vocabulary, stripped of the shallow jargon meanings of today's commercial marketplace. In my view, the term "structured analysis" which I coined and introduced in the 1974 AFCAM Final Report, should refer to the structured thinking and mode of expression that will indeed allow natural language to be the vehicle for perfect understanding.

APPENDIX

PRINCIPLES BEHIND THE RSA LANGUAGE

D. T. Ross

SofTech, Inc.

May 1979

9059-24

OBJECTIVES FOR RSA (ROSS' STRUCTURED ANALYSIS):
A SINGLE LANGUAGE FOR ALL SYSTEM THINKING
AND DOING.

OBJECTIVE OF THIS LECTURE:
TO SHOW HOW PERFECT UNDERSTANDING IS
POSSIBLE, WITH RSA.

TO HAVE ACCESS TO ANY AND ALL POSSIBLE SUBJECTS,
RSA MUST ACCEPT ANY NATURAL OR ARTIFICIAL
LANGUAGE AS A PROPER SUBSET.

IT DOES, BY REQUIRING ONLY SOME PAIR OF
OPPOSITES

THINGS	HAPPENINGS
NOUNS	VERBS
YIN	YANG
OPERATORS	OPERANDS

EVERY LANGUAGE HAS THESE, FOR THAT IS HOW
DISTINCTIONS, REFERENCES, CONNECTIONS ARE
MADE IN ANY LANGUAGE.

RSA ACCEPTS ANY LANGUAGE OPPOSITES AS

    NAMES   OF   BOXES

    LABELS   ON   ARROWS

SUCH THAT THE RSA BOX INTERFACES ARE VALID.

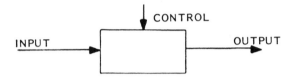

DEFINITION : M IS A MODEL OF SUBJECT S

    WITH RESPECT TO A QUESTION SET Q

    AND A TOLERANCE T

    IF M CAN BE USED TO ANSWER QUESTIONS ABOUT S,

$q_i \varepsilon$ Q, TO WITHIN T.

DEFINITION :

EVERY BOUNDARY WITHIN THE TOLERANCE

BAND IS EXACTLY THE NOMINAL BOUNDARY

(NOT "IS THE SAME AS...").

ANY BOUNDARY CAN BE MADE EXACT BY MAKING

ITS INNER AND OUTER BOUNDARIES EXACT.

THE SUBJECT, S, OF AN RSA MODEL IS BOUNDED
AND STRUCTURED BY ITS ORIENTATION:
    CONTEXT (WHERE IT IS SEEN FROM)
    VIEWPOINT (DETERMINES WHAT IS SEEN)
    PURPOSE (HOW IT IS SEEN)
THESE EMBODY QUESTION SET AND TOLERANCE.

TO BE UNDERSTOOD AT ALL, A SUBJECT MUST BE
DISTINCT FROM, BUT RELATED TO, SOMETHING
(EVERYTHING) ELSE.

IN RSA THE "EVERYTHING ELSE" IS BROKEN INTO
    OBJECT
    OBSERVER
    CONTEXT

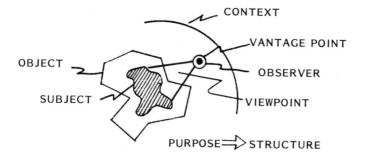

A SUBJECT IS AN ASPECT OF AN OBJECT WITH
RESPECT TO AN OBSERVER.

AN OBSERVER IS EMBEDDED IN (AND INCLUDED IN)
A CONTEXT (AT A VANTAGE POINT).

OBJECT EVINCES SUBJECT; CONTEXT EVICES SUBJECT.

FOR ORIENTATION: SUBJECT IS EVINCED BY OBJECT.

VIEWPOINT (DETERMINES WHAT IS SEEN) IS LIMITED
BY THE PERCEPTION OF THE OBSERVER.

UNDERSTANDING IS FURTHER LIMITED BY THE
CONCEPTION OF THE OBSERVER.

VIEWPOINT IS BOUNDED BY
    FIELD OF VIEW
    DEPTH OF FIELD
    WAVE LENGTH
AS IN OPTICS. THE SCENE IS WHAT IS SEEN.

A SUBJECT IS ACCESSED BY AN OBSERVER IN
    TERMS OF A LANGUAGE NATURAL TO THAT
    OBSERVER FOR THAT SUBJECT.

AN RSA MODEL HAS TWO COMPLEMENTARY, DUAL
    DECOMPOSITIONS (A.K.A. "MODELS")

MODELS:	DATA	ACTIVITY
THINGS	BOX	ARROW
HAPPENINGS	ARROW	BOX

BOTH COVER THE ENTIRE SUBJECT (SAME CONTEXT
    AND VIEWPOINT).

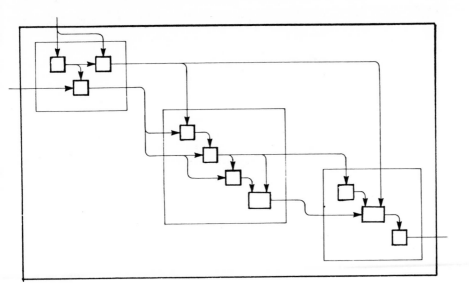

OUTER AND INNER BOUNDARIES

THE TOLERANCE OF AN RSA MODEL IS DETERMINED
    BY THE NATURAL LANGUAGE EXPRESSIONS
    LABELING ITS OUTER AND INNER BOUNDARIES.

THE OUTER BOUNDARY OF A MODEL IS THE INTERFACE
    BOUNDARY OF ITS LEVEL 0 BOX.

THE INNER BOUNDARY IS (COLLECTIVELY) THE
    INTERFACE BOUNDARIES OF ITS MOST DETAILED
    BOXES (THEMSELVES NOT DIRECTLY DETAILED).

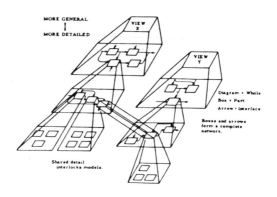

MULTIPLE MODELS IN RSA

HAVING SELECTED THE TYPE OF EMPHASIS, (ACTIVITY
OR DATA) A SINGLE BOX AT LEVEL 0 ENCOMPASSES
THE ENTIRE SUBJECT.

THE RSA MAXIM: "EVERYTHING WORTH SAYING ABOUT
ANYTHING WORTH SAYING SOMETHING ABOUT
MUST BE EXPRESSED IN SIX OR FEWER PIECES"
THEN ENSURES AN EXACT DECOMPOSITION.
(NO ADDITIONS, OMISSIONS, OR OVERLAPS).

THE RSA INTERFACE ARROWS (INPUT, CONTROL,
OUTPUT) INTERCONNECT BOXES IN EACH
DIAGRAM AND EACH DIAGRAM TO ITS (UNIQUE)
PARENT BOX (ENSURED BY ICOM CODES).

BY THE "EVERYTHING" RULE OF THE RSA MAXIM
THE OUTER AND INNER BOUNDARIES ARE
INTENDED TO BE THE SAME.

WITHOUT DETAILING, (I.E., ONE BOX ONLY) THEY
ARE THE SAME, BY DEFINITION, BUT THE
MEANING IS VERY UNCERTAIN.

WITH DETAILING, THEY DIFFER, BUT BOUND (BY
DEFINITION) EXACT NOMINAL MEANING,
WHICH STILL MAY BE VERY UNCERTAIN.

EACH STAGE OF FURTHER PURPOSEFUL DETAILING
MAKES THE OUTER, INNER, AND NOMINAL
MEANINGS LESS UNCERTAIN -- THE
STRUCTURING TIGHTENS THE TOLERANCE.

EVEN THOUGH THE NATURAL LANGUAGE TERMS MAY
HAVE MULTIPLE, AMBIGUOUS MEANINGS, MANY
ARE FORCED OUT OF CONSIDERATION BY THE
STRUCTURING.

PURPOSE (OF THE ORIENTATION OF THE MODEL)
DETERMINES THE STRUCTURE OF THE MODEL
BECAUSE EACH PARENT BOX BOUNDS THE
(SUB)CONTEXT OF ALL OFFSPRING BOXES.

IN THE TWO TYPES OF DECOMPOSITIONS (MODELS)

MODELS :	ACTIVITY	DATA
SUBSTANCE	INPUT-OUTPUT	CONTROL-OUTPUT
STRUCTURE	CONTROL	INPUT

THE STRUCTURE-DETERMINING ARROWS MUST BE SHOWN.

THE RSA EMBEDDING PRINCIPLE
LIMITS AND INTERCONNECTS THE POSSIBLE
SEMANTIC INTERPRETATIONS (MEANINGS) OF
THE NATURAL LANGUAGE NAMES AND LABELS
EMBEDDED IN AN RSA DECOMPOSITION (MODEL)
TO (ALL) THOSE THAT ARE ALLOWED BY THE
SYNTAX AND SEMANTICS OF THE GRAPHICAL
LANGUAGE EXPRESSION OF THE MODEL.

THE FUNDAMENTAL THEOREM OF RSA DECOMPOSITION:
RSA IMPROVES UNDERSTANDABILITY BY INCREASING
DETAIL OF DEFINITIONS AND DECREASING UNCERTAINTY
OF TERMS.

COROLLARY: OPTIMUM MODELING YIELDS MAXIMUM
    UNDERSTANDABILITY FOR A GIVEN ORIENTATION
    OF A SUBJECT.

EVENTUALLY THE DETAILING OF ANY RSA MODEL MUST
    REACH AN ATOMIC LEVEL OF ITS INNER BOUNDARY
    WHERE FURTHER DETAILING (FOR THAT ORIENTATION)
    IS IMPOSSIBLE.

THIS IS THE RSA FUNDAMENTAL LIMITATION OF VIEWPOINT.

AT THE ATOMIC LEVEL, EVERY OUTER BOUNDARY ARROW
    HAS BEEN MAXIMALLY UNRAVELLED (BY BRANCHES OR
    JOINS) AND EACH BRANCH TERMINATES ON AN
    ATOMIC BOX.

THE BOXES ALL ARE ATOMIC BECAUSE THEY CANNOT
BE FURTHER DECOMPOSED WITHOUT INTRODUCING
INTERNAL ARROWS FROM OUTSIDE THE CHOSEN
VIEWPOINT (ALL INTERNAL ARROWS ABOVE THE
ATOMIC LEVEL MUST HAVE BEEN IN THE VIEWPOINT).

THE FUNDAMENTAL LIMITATION IS NOT A LIMIT ON
THE SUBJECT NOR ON THE OBJECT THAT
EVINCES THE SUBJECT -- ONLY ON THE VIEWPOINT.

THE ATOMIC BOXES STILL ARE RICH WITH POTENTIAL
DETAIL AND STILL HARBOR MUCH UNCERTAINTY.
BUT THE MODEL ORIENTATION ALONE CANNOT
PENETRATE THE (FROM ITS VIEWPOINT) INDIVISIBLE
ATOMS.

TO PENETRATE THE ATOMIC LEVEL BOUNDARY, ONE
(OR) MORE ADDITIONAL SUPPORT MODEL(S) WITH
APPROPRIATE DIFFERENT ORIENTATION(S) MUST
BE INTRODUCED.

EACH SUCH SUPPORT MODEL PROVIDES A NEW
RSA LEVEL OF ABSTRACTION.

SUPPORT IS REPRESENTED IN RSA DIAGRAM LANGUAGE
BY AN UPWARD MECHANISM ARROW TO THE BOTTOM
OF THE RSA BOX:

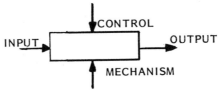

RSA MECHANISM SUPPORT IS A <u>CHANNEL OF CONNECTION</u>
BETWEEN ORIENTATIONS, <u>NOT</u> AN INTERFACE
BETWEEN PARTS OF A WHOLE.

IT ALLOWS ORIENTATIONS TO BE MIXED.

RSA ATOMS ARE <u>CONJUNCTIVE ATOMS</u> BECAUSE THEY
REQUIRE THAT MULTIPLE ORIENTATIONS BE
CONJOINED IN ORDER TO BE DETAILED.
WITH RESPECT TO THE ORIGINAL, PURE
ORIENTATION OF THE MODEL, THE SHARING
OF DETAILING WITH THE OTHER ORIENTATION(S)
TAKES PLACE AT A <u>SUBATOMIC LEVEL.</u>

EVERY CONJUNCTIVE ATOM BOX MUST HAVE AT LEAST
ONE SUPPORT CHANNEL ARROW THAT CONNECTS
TO AN UPWARD <u>SUPPLY</u> ARROW FROM THE TOP
OF SOME BOX OF A SUPPORTING MECHANISM
MODEL (USUALLY NOT THE LEVEL 0 BOX).

THE CONJUNCTIVE ATOM DETAIL DIAGRAM MUST THEN
HAVE AT LEAST ONE <u>RSA CALL</u> THROUGH A SUPPORT
CHANNEL TO A BOX OF A SUPPORT MODEL (USUALLY
NOT THE LEVEL 0 BOX, AND USUALLY NOT ANOTHER
(DEEPER) CONJUNCTIVE ATOM).

THE RSA CALL IS SIGNIFIED BY A DOWNWARD-ARROW
STUB FROM THE BOTTOM OF THE CALLING BOX.

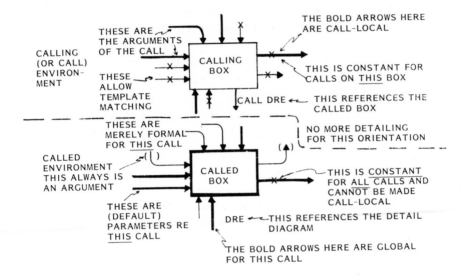

THE "TEMPLATE CALL" OF RSA

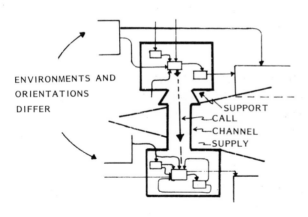

MECHANISMS SUPPLY SUPPORT

THE CALLED BOX MAY HAVE BOUNDARY ARROWS (I, C,
O, M) THAT ARE HIDDEN FROM CALLERS, AS
SIGNIFIED BY "X" ON THE ARROW SHANK.

EXCEPT FOR HIDDEN ARROWS, THE COMPLETE BOX
BOUNDARY (EXCEPT FOR THE CALL STUB) OF
THE CALLING BOX MUST EXACTLY MATCH THAT
OF THE CALLED BOX, BUT SOME ARROWS MAY BE
DUMMY STUBS, MARKED BY "X", SIGNIFYING THAT
THE CORRESPONDING CALLED BOX ARROW IS
INTENDED TO BE USED.

OTHERWISE THE CALLING BOX ARROWS ARE INTENDED
TO SUPPLANT THE CORRESPONDING CALLED BOX
ARROWS.

A COMPLETE CALLING BOX ARROW (NOT A STUB) WITH
AN "X" SUPPLANTS THE CALLED BOX ARROW, BUT
IS ITSELF HIDDEN TO ANY (OTHER) CALLS ON THE
CALLING BOX.

ANY CALLING BOX OR CALLED BOX BOUNDARY
ARROW MAY ALSO BE TUNNELLED AT EITHER THE
FREE END (GLOBAL CONNECTION) OR THE BOX
END (BLIND CONNECTION).

ALSO A CALLING BOX MAY HAVE POSITIVE NODE NUMBER
DETAILING WHICH ALLOWS A CALL TO HAVE MULTIPLE
MODEL PARAMETERS, ETC.

BUT FOR PURPOSES OF THIS LECTURE THOSE RSA FEATURES
ARE ADVANCED SECOND-ORDER REFINEMENTS.

THE IMPORTANT POINT IS THAT THE RESULTANT
RSA CALL BOUNDARY RIGOROUSLY JOINS THE
CALLING AND CALLED CONTEXTS ALLOWING
DETAILING OF THE CALLED BOX TO DECOMPOSE
THE MIXED ORIENTATION.

TOLERANCE FOR THE COMBINED MODEL (SUPPORTED
AND SUPPORTING) IS THEREFORE FURTHER
TIGHTENED.

SUCH INTRODUCTION OF EVER-DEEPER LEVELS OF
ABSTRACTION CAN, IN PRINCIPLE, CONTINUE
AND INFINITUM. HENCE THE INNER BOUNDARY
LIMITATION OF AN RSA MODEL CAN BE OVERCOME
TO ANY DESIRED DEGREE -- UP TO THE LIMITATION
STILL IMPOSED BY THE ORIGINAL LEVEL 0 BOX
OUTER (EXTERNAL) BOUNDARY.

THE OUTER BOUNDARY LIMITATION CAN SIMILARLY
BE OVERCOME TO ANY DESIRED DEGREE, AS
WELL, IN RSA BY DOUBLE PASSAGE THROUGH
THE DUAL DOMAIN, AS FOLLOWS.

JUST AS IN STANDARD DECOMPOSITION DETAILING
IT WAS NECESSARY TO PROCEED TO THE ATOMIC
LIMIT, AND THEN PENETRATE THAT BY NEW DEEPER
LEVELS OF ABSTRACTION IN ORDER TO UNRAVEL
THE INNER STRUCTURE OF THE EXTERNAL BOUNDARY
ARROWS TO ANY DESIRED DEGREE --

IT IS NECESSARY TO PROCEED TO HIGHER LEVELS
OF ABSTRACTION (INTO THE CONTEXT) IN ORDER
TO UNRAVEL THE OUTER STRUCTURE (SOURCES AND
SINKS AT SOME DESIRED ATOMICITY) OF THOSE SAME
EXTERNAL BOUNDARY ARROWS.

TO DO THIS, EACH LEVEL 0 EXTERNAL ARROW ITSELF
IS MODELLED IN THE DUAL DOMAIN AS A BOX THAT
IS DECOMPOSED ("UPWARD" AND DUAL), PERHAPS
WITH ADDITIONAL ABSTRACTION LEVELS, UNTIL
THE DESIRED ATOMICITY OF THE ORIGINAL "PIPELINE
CROSS-SECTION" IS REACHED.

AT THIS STAGE, THE ULTIMATE SOURCE OR SINK
TYPES OF ATOMIC-LEVEL UNRAVELLED BRANCHES
ARE KNOWN, BUT (BEING IN THE DUAL DOMAIN)
THE CORRESPONDING BOX ATOMS STILL MUST BE
FOUND.

THIS REQUIRES A CORRESPONDING SWITCH BACK TO THE
ORIGINAL (DUAL DUAL) DOMAIN, DEFINING THE
ATOMIC BOXES FIRST, THIS TIME. THESE ATOMIC
BOXES, SCATTERED LIKE A CONSTELLATION
THROUGHOUT THE ORIGINAL MODEL CONTEXT,
CONSTITUTE A NEW SUBJECT (EVINCED BY THE
CONTEXT IN RESPONSE TO THE DOUBLE DUAL
DOMAIN DEMANDS OF THE NEED FOR OUTER
STRUCTURING OF THE ORIGINAL EXTERNAL
BOUNDARY ARROWS).

FOR THIS TO
BE WHAT IT IS:

IT BROADCASTS
DEMANDS IN
D-MODELING OF
PIPELINE INTERFACES

TO ESTABLISH
THE DATA IT
NEEDS

THAT TERRITORY
IS A-MODELED TO
MATCH (WITH-NODE
NUMBERS)

AND THAT-A MODEL
PROVIDES THE
CONTEXT

IT MAY BE THE
ONLY CONTEXT
ALLOWING THAT
TO BE WHAT IT IS.

ESTABLISHING MODEL CONTEXT

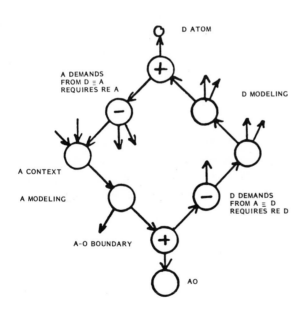

D ATOM

A DEMANDS
FROM D ≡ A
REQUIRES RE A

D MODELING

A CONTEXT

A MODELING

D DEMANDS
FROM A ≡ D
REQUIRES RE D

A-O BOUNDARY

AO

INTERFACE PIPELINES DRIVE CONTEXT MODELING

THIS SUBJECT THEN CAN BE BOX MODELLED (I.E.,
   IN THE SAME DOMAIN AS THE ORIGINAL), TO YIELD
   A NEGATIVE NODE NUMBERED CONTEXT MODEL
   (OR PERHAPS NETWORK OF MODELS AT STILL
   HIGHER LEVELS OF ABSTRACTION) SUCH THAT THE
   ORIGINAL MODEL (AND ITS DEEPER ABSTRACTION LEVELS)
   PROVIDES PROPER SUPPORT TO IT.

BY THIS PROCESS THE OUTER BOUNDARY MAY ALSO
   BE TIGHTENED ARBITRARILY.

THE CONTEXT MODEL IS A DESCRIPTIVE MODEL
   (NEGATIVE NODE NUMBERED) AS DISTINCT FROM
   STANDARD DETAILING DECOMPOSITION (ORDINARY
   NODE NUMBERING), WHICH IS DEFINITIVE MODELING.
   EVERY RSA BOX, CONSIDERED AS LEVEL 0 OF
   SOME MODEL, HAS SUCH A CONTEXT MODEL, IN
   PRINCIPLE. THE DESCRIPTIVE CONTEXT MODEL
   PRESCRIBES THE CONDITIONS A MODEL MUST MEET
   IN ORDER TO CALL ON THIS MODEL FOR SUPPORT.

AS MENTIONED, BUT NOT ELABORATED, RSA ALSO ALLOWS
   POSITIVE NODE NUMBERING, WHICH ALSO IS DESCRIPTIVE
   RATHER THAN DEFINITIVE, IN ORDER TO SIMILARLY
   PRESCRIBE THE CONDITIONS A MODEL MUST MEET
   IN ORDER TO SUPPLY SUPPORT (I.E., FILL IN
   DETAILS OF OR SPECIALIZE) THIS MODEL.

CONCLUSION: WITH THE INTRODUCTION AND INTEGRATION
(THROUGH CALL/SUPPORT) OF SUFFICIENT
PURPOSEFULLY STRUCTURED LEVELS OF ABSTRACTION,
THROUGH DEFINITIVE AND DESCRIPTIVE MULTIPLE
MODELS WITH APPROPRIATE ORIENTATIONS, THE
UNCERTAINTY OF INTENDED INTERPRETATION
(MEANING) OF ANY RSA MODEL MAY BE MADE AS
SMALL AS DESIRED, IN SPITE OF THE INHERENT
AMBIGUITY OF THE NATURAL LANGUAGE TERMS
USED IN THE MODELS.

PROPER STRUCTURAL MODELING IN THE SYNTAX AND
SEMANTICS OF RSA DIAGRAM LANGUAGE FORCES
ALL EXCEPT THE INTENDED MEANING OUT OF
CONSIDERATION.

BIBLIOGRAPHY

Air Force Materials Laboratory (July 1974). "Air Force Com-
    puter-Aided Manufacturing (AFCAM) Master Plan (Vol. II,
    App. A., and Vol. III)," Report No. AFML-TR-74-104, avail-
    able from DDC as AD 922-041L and 922-171L.
Canning, R. G. (July 1977). Getting the requirements right,
    EDP Analyzer 15(7).
Canning, R. G. (February 1978). Progress in software engi-
    neering: Part I, *EDP Analyzer 16(2)*.
Combelic, D. (1978). User experience with new software
    methods (SADT), *Proceedings of the National Computer Con-
    ference (AFIPS) 47*, 631-633.
Dickover, M. E., McGowan, C. L., and Ross, D. T. (1977).
    Software design using SADT, "Proceedings of the 1977
    Annual Conference of the Association for Computing Ma-
    chinery (ACM)," Seattle, Washington, October 16-19, 1977,
    125-133.
Feldmann, C., Schoman, K., and Snyder, R. (July 1975). Struc-
    tured analysis model for Naval Telecommunications Proce-
    dures Users Manual NTP3, "NRL Memorandum Report 3086,"
    Naval Research Laboratory.
Freeman, P. (1975). Towards improved review of software de-
    signs, *Proceedings of the National Computer Conference
    (AFIPS) 44*, 329-334.
Freeman, P., and Wasserman, A. I. (eds.) (1976). "Tutorial
    on Software Design Techniques," IEEE Catalog No. 76CH1145-
    2C.
Greenspan, S. J., and McGowan, C. L. (January 1978). Struc-
    turing software development for reliability, *Microelec-
    tronics and Reliability 17*, 75-84.
Hori, S. (1972). Human-directed activity cell model, "CAM-I
    Long-Range Planning Final Report," CAM-I, Inc.
Infotech State of the Art Report (1978). "Structured Analysis
    and Design (two volumes)," Infotech International Ltd.
    (available in USA from Auerbach Publishers, Inc.).
Irvine, C. A., and Morris, D. (February 1979). Requirements
    and design models: A case study, submitted to the 4th
    International Software Engineering Conference.

Melich, M. (1976). Evolution of naval missions and the naval tactical data system, "Proceedings of the Conference on Managing the Development of Weapons System Software," 26-1 - 26-36.

Pederson, J. T., and Buckle, J. K. (July 1978). Kongsberg's road to an industrial software methodology, *IEEE Transactions on Software Engineering 4(4)*, 263-269.

Ross, D. T. (1961). A generalized technique for symbol manipulation and numerical calculation, Presented at the ACM Conference on Symbol Manipulation, Philadelphia, May 20-21, 1960, and published in *Communications of the ACM 4(3)*, 63-65.

Ross, D. T. (1971). It's time to ask why?, Guest Editorial, *Software Practice and Experience I(January-March)*, 103-104.

Ross, D. T. (May 1974). Structured analysis, "Proceedings International CAM Congress," CAM-I, Inc.

Ross, D. T. (November 1975). "Plex 1: Sameness and the Need for Rigor," SofTech Document No. 9031-1.1.

Ross, D. T. (December 1975). "Plex 2: Sameness and Type," SofTech Document No. 9031-2.

Ross, D. T. (1976). Toward foundations for the understanding of type, Conference on Data, March 22-24, 1976, Salt Lake City, Utah, "ACM SIGPLAN Notices," Vol. II, Special Issue, 63-65.

Ross, D. T. (January 1976). "Some Further Observations about Structured Analysis," SofTech Document No. 9031-6.1.

Ross, D. T. (April 1976). "are: pres.pl. of BE.," SofTech Document No. 9031-10.

Ross, D. T. (January 1977). Reflections on requirements, Guest Editorial, *IEEE Transactions on Software Engineering 3(1)*, 2-5.

Ross, D. T. (January 1977). Structured analysis (SA): A language for communicating ideas, *IEEE Transactions on Software Engineering 3(1)*, 16-34.

Ross, D. T. (October 1977). "Theoretical Foundations for Characterization," Integrated Computer-Aided Manufacturing (ICAM) Task II Final Report, Vol. II, SofTech Document No. 1033-7V2.

Ross, D. T. (1978). Quality starts with requirements definition, IFIP Working Conference on Constructing Quality
Software, Novosibirsk, USSR, May 23-28, 1977. "Constructing Quality Software," P. G. Hibbard and S. A. Schuman
(eds.), IFIP, North-Holland Publishing Company, 397-406.

Ross, D. T. (February 1979). "Structured Analysis (RSA):
The Big Picture of Design," SofTech Document No. 9059-21.

Ross, D. T. (March 1979). "Plex 4: Understanding Understanding," SofTech Document No. 9059-22.

Ross, D. T. (May 1979). "Structured Analysis (RSA): Design
Language Roadmaps," SofTech Document No. 9059-23.

Ross, D. T. (October 1979). "Removing the Limitations of
Natural Language," SofTech Document No. 9061-25.

Ross, D. T., and Brackett, J. W. (September 1976). An approach to structured analysis, *Computer Decisions 8(9)*,
40-44.

Ross, D. T., Goodenough, J. G., and Irvine, C. A. (May 1975).
Software engineering, process, principles, and goals,
Computer, 17-27.

Ross, D. T., and Munck, R. G. (February 1977). "Geometric
Modeling in Computer-Aided Manufacturing," SofTech Document No. 9037-13.

Ross, D. T., and Schoman, K. E. (January 1977). Structured
analysis for requirements definition, *IEEE Transactions
on Software Engineering 3(1)*, 6-15.

SofTech, Inc. (May 1976). "TRAIDEX Needs and Implementation
Study," DARPA Contract No. MDA 903-75-C-0224, available
from NTIS as AD-A-024-861.

SofTech, Inc. (November 1976). "An Introduction to SADT,"
SofTech Document No. 9022-78R.

SofTech, Inc. (June 1977). "Task 3 Report: The Army Training and Evaluation System," DARPA Contract No. MDA 903-76-
C-0249, available from NTIS as AD-B-020-656L.

Wisnosky, D. E. (February 1977). ICAM: The Air Force's
integrated computer-aided manufacturing program, *Astro-
nautics & Aeronautics 15*, 52-59.

Wisnosky, D. E. (April 1977). Using computers to improve
manufacturing productivity, *Defense Management Journal
13(2)*, 41-50.

Zimmerman, M. D. (May 1977). ICAM: Revolution in manufacturing, *Machine Design 49(12)*, 2-7.

LANGUAGE ASPECTS OF SOFTWARE ENGINEERING[1]

Jean E. Sammet

Federal Systems Division
IBM Corporation
Bethesda, Maryland

INTRODUCTION

The purpose of this paper is to give the author's personal view, and a general indication of the language aspects of software engineering. In order to do this, it is necessary for me to provide my own definition of software engineering so that readers will understand the approach and concepts that I am using.

> "Software Engineering is the set of
> disciplines, tools and techniques (both
> technical and nontechnical) needed
> (and/or used) to produce efficient,
> correct, reliable ...
>
> < any adjective denoting good >
> software in a manner which is timely,
> and is cost effective over the entire
> life cycle of the software."

Using the above definition, or for that matter almost any other, it is clear that software engineering has two

---

[1] *A slight modification of this paper will form one section of a paper dealing with programming languages to appear in Volume 20 of Advances in Computers, published by Academic Press.*

components - a management aspect and a technical aspect.
This paper deals only with a subset of the technical aspect,
namely that involving languages.

By now there are almost as many definitions of the life
cycle of program development as there are people who wish to
prepare such a list. In compliance with fairly commonly
accepted lists, I consider the major steps to be: requirements definition, specification definition, designing, coding,
testing, documenting, verifying, and maintaining. It is not
the purpose of this paper to debate the merits of this particular list but rather simply to use that list as the
launching point for discussing the various aspects of languages. (Generally the first two steps involve the problem
definition, the next three produce the problem solution, and
the last three involve the practical use of the actual software.)

The term "languages" as used in this paper covers a wide
spectrum of types of languages, and it is beyond the scope of
this paper to define that spectrum except by examples or
discussions. Only some of the steps involve what are commonly considered as "programming languages" (exemplified by
FORTRAN and COBOL).

The following table lists the steps in the life cycle and
the importance of languages currently and for the future. The

Activity	Current status	Future status	Future relevance of high level languages
Requirements definition	L - M	M	O
Specification definition	L - M	M - H	O
Design	M	H	M
Code	H	H	H
Test	L	L	L
Document	M	M	M
Verify	L - M	H	M
Maintain	L - M	M - H	M

"Current Status" and "Future Status" columns involve whatever
type of language is most appropriate to that phase of the
life cycle (as discussed in the following sections). The
last column specifically refers to the future relevance of
what are currently considered the common types of high level
languages to the indicated step in the life cycle. The
letters H, M and L and the number 0 stand for high, medium,
low, and not relevant, respectively; where an upgrading for
the current status to the future status is shown, this means
that in my opinion a change will occur; even more importantly
there is a need for research and development to cause that
change to take place.

LANGUAGE INVOLVEMENT IN THE LIFE CYCLE STEPS

Requirements Definition

The matter of stating the requirements for a particular
problem which is to be solved on a computer is often more a
matter of psychology, and perhaps clairvoyance, than technology. (However, in spite of that somewhat cynical statement,
a fair amount of research has been and is being carried out,
and hopefully will continue to be done in terms of the requirements.) In the simplest form, one would like merely to
say to a computer "calculate the payroll" or "calculate the
most effective route to fly from New York to Los Angeles".
Of course, in neither one of these is the information provided
anywhere near sufficient for even the most science-fiction
dreams of computers to provide answers, simply because there
is not adequate information even for humans to solve the problem. In the case of the payroll, one needs to provide the
data for each employee along with such basic facts as whether
the payroll is generated weekly, semimonthly, or monthly,
whether people are paid in cash or by check, and what reports
must be provided to the IRS, etc. In the case of the air
route the definition of "best" is certainly ambiguous. It
might mean speediest, or smoothest for the passengers, or
most economical from the point of view of fuel expenditure;
these details on the requirements must be specified. In an

ideal world, once the individual had simply stated his
general conceptual requirement, the system should be knowledgeable enough to ask all the right questions. Naturally,
we are a long way off from that, and even if the correct
answers were provided to define the problem clearly, there
could still be a large gap until the problem solution were
obtained.

The type of research that is going on in this area
generally comes under the heading of the phrase "automatic
programming". In the early days of computers (circa 1950's)
the phrase "automatic programming" merely meant any tool or
technique which was easier for the programmer to use than
coding in octal or binary or with absolute machine addresses.
The terms "automatic coding" and "automatic programming" were
often used interchangeably, and in both cases tended to mean
some form of language that was easier to use than absolute
machine language. In today's environment, automatic programming tends to have two major subcategories - one is referred
to as "general systems" while the other is referred to as
"knowledge-based systems". In the case of knowledge-based
systems, it is assumed that the system is built containing
specific information that is relevant to a particular application or class of applications (e.g., airline reservations);
that is, the domain of application is restricted. By way of
contrast, the general systems have allegedly within them the
capability of asking for and receiving information on a
number of applications. The system then uses general control
structures to deal with the specific application. If these
concepts sound amorphous, it is because this is still in an
early stage of research.

Specification Definition

There is considerable debate concerning the distinctions
between requirements and specifications; some people combine
the concepts for the purpose of life-cycle definition. The
distinction I would make here is that the specifications are
meant to be much more detailed than they would be in a
requirements statement, even if the latter did have considerable detail. Thus, for example, in the case of the payroll

one might answer all of the questions listed above (as well
as others) to provide all the requirements, but the specifications would be more rigorously and rigidly stated with
considerably more detail (e.g., showing output formats). In
some instances, the borderline between requirements and
specifications is not very clear.

There are some languages and/or systems being used for
defining specifications, for example the PSL/PSA work done at
the University of Michigan [Teichroew and Hershey (1977)].
(PSL/PSA is often referred to as a requirements language
rather than a specifications language.)

A major aspect of the specification languages is the
potential (and necessity) for tying in to both design and
verification. Obviously, in order to design a program one
must know the specifications. The difference is that the
specifications indicate what is to be done and the design
(discussed in the next section) should indicate how it is to
be done within the specific physical constraints available to
the designer. However, since the design must reflect the
specifications, any relationship between those languages must
be carefully understood.

The connection between specifications and verification is
even more important. Obviously, if one is going to verify a
program, then one needs a base point against which to provide
and perform this verification. Clearly one can only verify
against what was intended. In our current terminology the
most likely place at which to measure or indicate what is
intended is in the specifications. (It is necessary to
assume the specifications are correct or else the verification becomes meaningless.) It would be more desirable to be
able to tie back to the requirements but this is undoubtedly
impossible, and certainly so difficult as to be beyond compre-
hension at this time in the state of the art.

The specification languages should have two characteristics which are needed to reflect their major intersection
with the users. On one hand the specifications should be
natural to the specific application user, and on the other
hand they should be readable by a wider variety of people.
The reason that these are cited as two different

characteristics is because there are potentially two different
audiences involved. Obviously if the user is going to look
at the specifications to see whether they really meet his
needs, then the material must be in a notation that is
natural to him. On the other hand many people besides the
users will need to work with these specifications, for
example, the program designers. Furthermore as indicated
above, those people trying to verify the final program will
need to come back to the specifications. And if they are
unable to read the specifications, then obviously they will
not be able to verify that the program meets them. (Note that
being natural and being readable are not the same thing if two
different audiences are involved.)

Designing

A significant amount of work has been done in the development
of "process design" languages or "program design"
languages. In fact the initials PDL are generic but also
specific for certain languages [Linger, Mills and Witt (1979);
Caine and Gordon (1975)]. In this context PDL as a generic
term means some semi-formal notation that allows people to
indicate the design of a program but without actually doing
the final coding. Many of the process/program design
languages allow and/or encourage stepwise refinement and
continual verifiability. They do this by essentially allowing a portion of the program to be written in a formal notation but also allow another portion of it to be written in
any language that is natural and convenient to the designer.
For example, one can write

```
WHILE

    socsectax  <  maxvalue

DO

    deduct socsectax

ENDDO
```

where the words WHILE, DO and ENDDO are part of the formal
notation, and the lower-case words represent any process
description the designer desires.

There is a significant but unresolved problem of how to
interface between the design languages and the executable
languages. In some cases, the former are just as formal as
the latter, or could easily be made so. But the programmer
must go through a relatively mechanical step of converting
and hand-translating the design language to the "normal"
high-level language that can be compiled into machine code.

For reasons similar to those given above it is important
that the design languages be natural and readable to some
(although not necessarily all) of the end users and programmers.

Coding

In some discussions of the life cycle or the entire program development process, the word "programming" is used
rather than "coding". When "programming" is used it usually
is meant to encompass at least part (if not all) of the design process. Since part of the basic point of this discussion is clearly to delineate different steps in the life
cycle, it is quite appropriate to use the word "coding" to
mean the specific steps of writing down a program that can
be put into a computer for eventual execution.

A major aspect of the programming language relationship
to software engineering involves the term "structured programming"; this is another one of those phrases that has
almost as many meanings as there are people. In this context
I mean that there is only a small set of allowable control
structures that exist in the programming language. Normally
this set would include (a) sequential statements, (b) some
type of loop statement (which might be "WHILE ... DO ..." or
"FOR I = ... DO ...") and (c) some branch statement, usually
denoted by "IF ... THEN ... ELSE ...", all with the general
constraint of flow paths allowing only one entry and one exit.

In order to obtain the maximum benefits of the "engineering" aspect of "software engineering" the coding should be
done in a high level language such as COBOL, FORTRAN, PL/I,

etc. This generally provides the characteristic of having a
readable program in order to ease debugging and other steps
(e.g., documentation) in the life cycle. The report [Shaw
et al (1978)] compares portions of COBOL, FORTRAN, JOVIAL,
and the IRONMAN [DOD (1977)] requirements for issues those
authors deem significant from a software engineering viewpoint.

Another possible approach to coding is to devise high
level languages that are natural to the problem area of the
user, although they are quite different from the more common
high level languages. These are what I have referred to
[Sammet (1972)] as "languages for specialized application
areas" or "specialized application languages". The most
common examples are COGO (COordinate GeOmetry) for civil
engineers, and APT (Automatically Programmed Tools) for
numerically controlled machine tools. The advantages of
these languages are that it is possible to obtain readability
and naturalness at the same time because of the close connection between the language itself and the field of application.

Testing

This has a low relationship to programming languages
although obviously testing is extremely important in the life
cycle. But aside from including in a specific language certain features that make the testing easier, and aside from
the development of languages to help generate test cases,
there is not much of a connection. This does not mean that
testing is unimportant; on the contrary, there is a lot of
consideration being given to this subject (see for example
Goodenough (1979)) but most of the issues are not particularly
related to languages. For example, the question of how fully
testing can and should be done is not a language issue.

It is worth noting for the reader who may be unfamiliar
with this general subject that testing and validation/verifi-
cation are not the same. Definition of these terms and a
delineation of the differences are beyond the scope of this
paper.

Documenting

It is clear, on one hand, that each of the steps above
need documentation, in the sense of describing and/or explain-
ing the formalism that is written down. On the other hand,
to the extent that what is written down is readable, then it
is self documenting to that same extent. Furthermore if it
were possible to have a sequence of actions in which the
requirements statements could be directly translated to
specification statements, which could then in turn be
directly translated into the design, and then into the code,
then we would have self documentation at any desired level.

Verifying

This is a very controversial subject, and I do not want
to get involved in the discussion of how or when programs can
be verified and to what level, nor whether or not such verification is important. My concern here is only with indicating
the relationship to programming languages. Now some of this
has already been mentioned earlier, in the sense that if the
specifications are clearly written and can be automatically
(or at least semi-automatically) translated down into executable code, then the verification becomes very much easier.
However, this seems to be beyond the current state of the
art. We, therefore, have two types of approaches. One is
to include in existing programming languages certain additional statements or features to make them more easily verifiable. The other, which is certainly a topic of great research
these days, is to develop specific (new) languages that are
designed with easy verifiability in mind. (EUCLID [Lampson
et al (1977)] is a language designed with that objective.)
The flaw in this concept as far as I am concerned, is that
one really must verify the code itself. Thus if a specification says to produce 10 copies of a report, then the language
should make it easy to verify that the code written will in
fact produce 10 copies.

Maintaining

The word "maintenance" covers several aspects of program development, namely correction of bugs, correction of design deficiencies, and enhancement. In each case, the relationship of programming languages to the indicated task depends entirely on the material discussed above, that is, the language elements in earlier steps of the life cycle. If there were adequate languages in each preceding step, then maintenance could often be done in such a way as to update everything at the same time.

OTHER ISSUES INVOLVING HIGH LEVEL LANGUAGES

Reliability

There is naturally great concern about developing languages that make it easy to produce reliable programs. There are unfortunately no facts (or at least none that I can discern) pertaining to this matter, and the issue seems to involve matters of personal judgment more than anything else. Thus some special features which can be required in a language, and which allegedly lead to more reliability are based on the personal judgment that a particular style will lead to more reliable programs. Thus, for example, there are people who argue that more reliable programs will be produced if the language requires that all data be declared and no defaults are allowed, or people who insist on strong typing and allow absolutely no implicit conversion as a means of producing more reliable programs. While I tend to agree with many of these viewpoints, I also recognize the validity of a counterargument that says that when you make the programmer write more and when you force him to do things which could be done implicitly by the compiler, that you have not improved reliability. Similarly, special languages have been developed which the designers claim provide more reliability (see for example [ACM SIGPLAN (1977)].

While many of these issues are still (in my opinion) matters of individual professional judgment, fortunately there has been some work in attempting to provide valid experimental data on which language features seem to cause

higher (or lower) programmer error rates. See for example,
[Gannon (1977)] and the references in that paper, as well as
numerous related papers in the proceedings containing [Gannon
and Horning (1975)].

Portability

   Inherent in any concept of software engineering is the
potential need for portability, that is, the ability to move
a running program from one computer to another, or to get the
same results using different compilers for the translation.
The reason that this is a fundamental concept is that installations change their needs and requirements, and, therefore,
any program that has been developed with portability as an
objective should be able to be moved with little or no effort.
(This is great in theory; the effort often turns out to be
considerable in practice!)

   Now the major concern of most people is, of course, portability across physical computers, where in this context it
is assumed that we are talking about machines of different
architectures and/or different order codes. (I am specifically not referring to a family of upward compatible machines.) The need to move programs across machines has been
well known and well understood almost from the very beginning
of major use of computers. However, what seems to be much
less well known - although it is in fact more important - is
the problem of portability across compilers. This point
deserves amplification, for the simple reason that compilers
are changed more often than machines. (Updates to operating
systems can hamper portability as well, but that problem is
not germane to this discussion unless there are commensurate
difficulties with the compiler.)

   Most vendors who produce a compiler try to produce a
better one than their previous version or than their competi-
tors'. But this often plays havoc with a source program.
Part of the reason is that many of our languages do not have
rigorous definitions, and even for those that do, there is no
assurance that the compiler actually complies with the definition. Even though there are many formal techniques for
defining the syntax and semantics of programming languages

[Marcotty and Ledgard (1976)], few (if any) compiler writers are able to use formal language definitions in a way that guarantees that the compiler complies with them. Put still another way, verifying a compiler is the same conceptually as verifying any program. One needs to look at the compiler and see whether it meets its specifications; in this case the specifications are the language definition. I do not believe that there has been any substantial case of compiler verification. There have been small or experimental instances of such work, but those are inadequate for a production environment. For all these reasons a "new" compiler may cause previously correct programs to become invalid.

Another area of lack of portability to a new compiler occurs when a compiler which implements a standard language also adds and provides additional features so that the user rapidly becomes accustomed to this unexpected luxury which is not present in the standard language. A new compiler may not provide those same luxuries, or, more commonly, may provide a different set of luxuries, thus rendering the original programs unusable. Finally, many compilers depend on an operating system and the programmer discovers this and uses that information in his program, which reduces portability. Furthermore the changes in an operating system may be subtle and hence difficult to detect.

In order to achieve portability across computers, there should be little or no machine-dependent features and elements in the program and/or language. This is far easier to say than to accomplish. While there are certain obvious issues (e.g., word length which affects the accuracy of any numerical computation), and even moderately obvious ones (e.g., collating sequence, which affects the way in which tests of non-numeric inequality are carried out), there are more subtle issues, (e.g., whether zero is treated as positive or negative or unsigned).

As with so many other things in the computer field, one can achieve portability if one is willing to pay a price in efficiency. One example, and an extreme case, would occur if a language had a command which allowed one to read a

magnetic tape in reverse order. If the programmer writes a
program with that command and then moves the program to
another machine that does not have that hardware capability,
it can, of course, be simulated by rewinding a tape and reading forward one less record than before. It is certainly
unlikely, and probably inconceivable, that such inefficiency
would be tolerated.

SUMMARY AND CONCLUSIONS

In most steps of the life cycle of software development
there are language aspects. The major step (in 1979)
affected by languages is clearly the actual coding which involves the commonly used high level languages. Other steps
which are moderately affected by languages are design and
documentation. It is expected that in the future, the design
step will be as strongly affected by programming languages as
is direct coding now, with specification languages not far
behind. It is also expected that in the future the relationship between programming languages and verification will
become much greater than it is now.

REFERENCES

ACM SIGPLAN (March 1977). Proc. ACM Conference on Language
    Design for Reliable Software, *ACM SIGPLAN Notices 12(3)*.
Caine, Stephen H., and Gordon, E. Kent (1975). PDL - A Tool
    for Software Design, *AFIPS Conf. Proc. NCC 44*.
Dept. of Defense, High Order Language Working Group (Jan.
    1977). "Department of Defense Requirements for High-
    Order Computer Programming Languages: 'Ironman'", Depart-
    ment of Defense.
Gannon, J. D. (August 1977). An experimental evaluation of
    data type conventions, *Comm. ACM 20(8)*.
Gannon, J. D., and Horning, J. J. (June 1975). The impact
    of language design on the production of reliable software,
    Proc. International Conference on Reliable Software, *ACM
    SIGPLAN Notices 10(6)*.

Goodenough, John B. (1979). A survey of program testing
    issues, *In* "Research Directions in Software Technology,"
    (Peter Wegner, ed.), MIT Press, Cambridge, Mass.
IEEE Computer Society (1979). Proc. Conference on Specifica-
    tions of Reliable Software, IEEE Catalog No. 79 CH1401-9C,
    IEEE Computer Society, P. O. Box 639, Silver Springs, MD
    20901.
Lampson, B. W., Horning, J. J., London, R. L., Mitchell, J. G.
    and Popek, G. L. (Feb. 1977). Report on the programming
    language Euclid, *ACM SIGPLAN Notices 12(2)*.
Linger, Richard C., Mills, Harlan D., and Witt, Bernard I.
    (1979). "Structured Programming: Theory and Practice,"
    Addison-Wesley, Reading, Mass.
Marcotty, Michael, and Ledgard, Henry F. (June 1976). A
    sampler of formal definitions, *ACM Computing Surveys 8(2)*.
Sammet, Jean E. (1972). An overview of programming languages
    for specialized application areas, *AFIPS Conf. Proc. SJCC
    40*.
Shaw, Mary, Almes, Guy T., Newcomer, Joseph M., Reid, Brian
    K., and Wulf, Wm. A. (April 1978). "A Comparison of
    Programming Languages for Software Engineering," Carnegie-
    Mellon Univ., Dept. of Computer Science, CMU-CS-78-119.
Teichroew, D., and Hershey, E. A. (Jan. 1977). PSL/PSA: A
    computer-aided technique for structured documentation and
    analysis of information processing systems, *IEEE Trans.
    on Software Engineering SE-3(1)*.

THE IMPACT OF TECHNOLOGY ON SOFTWARE

D. Tsichritzis

Computer Systems Research Group
University of Toronto
Toronto, Canada

INTRODUCTION

In the "good old times" computers were really expensive.
Their cost overshadowed any other expense. Their users were
few and very knowledgeable. Their priests were very talented.
Any idiosynchrasy in their operation was attributed to efficiency goals in their use. Their applications were well understood. We could afford to waste some systems programmers'
creative talents to babysit with computers and bend people's
needs and tastes to accommodate machines. Unfortunately computers are getting cheaper. While this solves many old problems, it creates, or rather makes visible, some rather nasty
new ones. We were getting used to solving the old problems.
Unfortunately, their solutions do not provide us with any insight about handling the new ones. The old problems were
mainly machine problems. They were better defined. The new
problems are people-plus-machine problems. They are difficult to pin down, let alone solve. We will soon have the
capability of putting a phenomenal amount of computing power
at everybody's disposal for a small cost. The problem is to
explore ways in which this power can be used effectively.

When computers were very expensive, their use was carefully controlled and their resource allocation heavily optimized. The computer service was centered around a general-
purpose computer. Extensive floor space and manpower was committed to the translation of raw computer power into many
different services. Many diversified applications were

forcibly brought together because they had to share a common
machine. As a result, computer centers became an all-encompassing tool but also a major burden.

On the other hand, where computers are cheap, they can
proliferate. They can migrate to exactly where they are
needed. Duplication of hardware is then not a major problem.
It is more important to optimize the use of personnel and
floor space. There is no need to try to understand everybody's problems in order to solve them with the big machine.
If we provide the end users with the right tools, they can
determine the best way to deal with their problems.

The low cost of computers today allows us to break up
general-purpose computer systems into small functional units.
However, it is often very difficult to decide what these functional units should be. We should not simply look inside
present computer systems and try to isolate their functional
modules, such as compilers, data base systems, etc. That
could point us in the wrong direction. Present computer systems were designed to serve a specific environment. Since
the environment has changed, both they and their function are
subject to change. We should look instead to the end uses
of computers and investigate their different characteristics.
We are not interested in describing the exact way that computer services should be provided. There are a wide range of
solutions according to different needs and operational environments. We are interested only in the directions that the
solutions may take and the kind of systems we may end up with.
This in turn has some relevance to the kind of software we
will need.

COMPUTER USAGE

We can classify computer services into two groups: services to people of an organization and services to the organization's needs. Most people in an organization have simple
needs usually provided by office systems. They need to process documents, to have access to design and analysis tools,
to store and retrieve data, etc. We will refer to these needs
as *personal computing services*. Note that personal computing

services have little to do with computation. Very few people need computational power which can not be provided by a cheap calculator. Personal computing services deal mainly with information processing. That is, they provide a flexible and simple-to-use environment to obtain, store, digest and create information. Personal computing services manipulate data which is predominantly local. They produce results which have for the most part local flavor and value. For example, text editors, interactive packages, etc. are used for personal computing services.

The needs of the organization are provided by *organization computing services*. These are services which work on large sets of global data. They produce results that benefit the organization as a whole. These results may be directed toward a few people, e.g., management. However, these people have access to the results not as people but as actors playing a role in the organization. Their needs and the benefit of their actions are related to the organization as a whole. For example, payroll systems, inventory control systems, etc. provide organization computing services.

The distinction between personal and organization computing services is necessarily blurred. After all, if we serve the organization's people we serve the organization and vice versa (hopefully). The distinction can be clarified by a hypothetical situation. Suppose we place, temporarily, the entire computer center of an organization at an average person's disposal. Anything he would require in order better to perform his/her job we call personal computing services. Anything else that the computer center does for the benefit of the organization is organization computing services.

There is a third area, where personal and organization computing services blend together. This area will be loosely called *interaction services*. People use interaction services to communicate with other people. These services satisfy personal needs. They could, therefore, be classified as personal computing services. Since they are provided, however, in a global fashion, they could also be thought of as organization services. As a matter of fact, interaction services can be provided in two distinct ways. In one way, we have a

global data base where users can deposit or retrieve information. Using the common data base they can interact strongly
with each other. This is more of an organization computing
service. The common information can also be used for other
global processing. In the other way, we can have a message
system which users utilize to send messages to each other.
This is more of a personal service. The user views this service as mainly satisfying his needs and not as any global
organization necessity. However, message systems are provided
in a uniform manner as a tool for the organization as a whole.

Personal computing services, organization computing services and interaction services can be provided all together in
terms of a general-purpose, time-sharing system. The user can
access the system through a terminal for personal computing
services. Global organization needs are satisfied by the same
centralized system. Finally, interaction services are provided through process communication and file sharing. This
combination of different services is dictated by the cost of
hardware and the need for its efficient utilization.

In general-purpose systems there is a distinction between
batch and on-line systems. This distinction deals mainly with
the way the services are provided and not their function.
Batch jobs relate mainly to organization computing services.
A person, however, may also submit an analysis problem as a
batch job. Hence, some batch jobs may correspond to personal
computing services. On-line activity has three components.
It has a personal services component since that is the only
way that some personal services can be offered, e.g., a person doing text editing. On-line systems provide the means for
heavy interaction between users. Finally, on-line systems
have some organization services which can also be thought of
as interaction services. For instance, a reservation transaction benefits the organization but basically provides an interaction facility. One of the reasons that general-purpose
systems are so complex is that they mix different kinds of
services. A second reason is that they try to provide all
these diversified services while optimizing their resource allocation. Actually, the optimization of their resources is a
fourth and major service which they provide for themselves and
which competes with the other, user-oriented, services.

If the cost of hardware is not an overriding factor, services can be unbundled. It seems reasonable to separate personal computing services and provide them by, what else, personal computers. Organization computing services can be retained by large centralized systems. Interaction services can be provided by a combination of both centralized and decentralized systems. As a matter of fact, interaction services now become very important. They are no longer implicit and provided "de facto" due to the existence of a common host. They are explicit and need special hardware, in terms of networks, and software, in terms of message systems. On the other hand, interaction is purely positive. It does not imply interference or unwanted interaction forced by the use of common computing resources. It is interaction, when and if, the users want it.

PERSONAL COMPUTING SERVICES

In the previous section we separated, conceptually, personal computing services and argued that they can be provided in a decentralized fashion. First, let us observe that a decentralized system can be visualized as the result of breaking up and distributing some of the resources of a centralized system among the users' stations. This operation is carried out so as to completely separate the resources needed for personal services. To propose this decentralization as a realistic solution we should think about individual components of the centralized system and argue the merits of their distribution. We will discuss, therefore, decentralization of four types of resources - processors, main memory, secondary storage and peripherals. In addition, we will comment on the effects of the decentralization on communications, coordination and control, personnel and services, and finally the real target of this paper, software.

In a centralized system a large processor is time-sliced among the users. The processor allocation is very dynamic and flexible. In the decentralized system the processing power is statically allocated and very inflexible. With microprocessors, however, it makes sense completely to separate

the processors. We lose in flexibility and the availability
of a large processing unit. However, we gain in simplicity
of operation. In addition, processing is becoming so cheap
that underutilizing it is not that critical. The only real
waste is that the personal processors at the user's site are
completely idle when the user does not use them. This can be
remedied by providing real microprocessors (as opposed to
virtual machines) to a user via a switching system. Alterna-
tively, given a room containing many not-so-personal microprocessors, users can walk in and use an available one. In
summary, processing power can be provided for personal services by using personal computers, as opposed to virtual ones
through a large time-shared system.

Memory is more expensive than processing. We can, of
course, centralize the memory and dynamically allocate it to
a set of processors. However, memory itself is getting cheap
enough so that we do not need to worry too much about its
utilization. It is far simpler and more natural to associate
the memory with each processor. We end up with a network of
real processors with real memory connected together. Note
that by memory we mean any kind of memory that is not rotating
storage. To the extent that monolithic memory, bubbles or
CCD's become realistic alternatives for providing inexpensive
Mbytes of memory, we will look on them as memory to be associated with a personal processor.

By secondary storage we imply disk-type storage. Disks
are not cheap enough to be distributed widely. We can argue
that they will never be very cheap because they are sensitive
electromechanical devices. In addition, the cost per byte for
large disks is less than for small disks. Thus we have at
least one kind of device that should not be widely distributed.
Disks do not work by themselves. We need some processing and
memory to drive them. A small computer with a large disk can
provide disk space for many users. In this way disk space is
clustered and can be used by many personal computers.

Other peripherals are also clustered. We do not envision
a printer in everybody's office. A printer is not only expensive, but also bothersome. Printers should be where people
find it easy to access them. For example, in a room within

easy walking distance. In addition, there may be other not-
commonly-used devices that may be clustered and shared among
users.

Communication among all these machines can be via local
networks, global networks, multiplexed telephone lines, fiber
optics, etc. Communications are evolving so rapidly that they
provide us with many exciting alternatives. There are no
binding restrictions in terms of communications.

Maintenance of a decentralized system should pose no great
difficulty. Suppose we are dealing with a homogeneous system
of personal computers using common software. It is no harder
to service both the hardware and the software in this system
than in a centralized operation. Personal computers should
not require any more hardware maintenance than do terminals.
The common software can be maintained centrally. There is no
need for operators, except perhaps for the printer clusters
and the disk storage machines.

Our arguments point to a system architecture for personal
computing services where a number of small personal processors
with their own memory are tied together through a network. In
addition, there are common processors that manage disk storage
and other peripherals.

We cannot claim at this point that such a system will provide cheaper personal computing services than a time-sharing
system. The cost differential, however, is not very great.
In such a case, the feeling of ownership and freedom from
arbitrary computer center actions provided by a decentralized
system will justify the cost difference. As an analogy, cars
are not the cheapest way for people to move around. However,
people will use them as long as they are more convenient and
not unreasonably more expensive than public transportation.
In the long run personal computers are likely to win the economic argument as well: they will become cheaper simply because they will be produced in much larger volumes than large
machines.

We shall now concentrate on the software directions in
such an environment of personal computing services. The hardware architecture of individual machines can be assumed to be
basically similar. This implies that there is no need to

change any of the system software running on the personal
computers. This is true for individual software components
like compilers, editors, etc. However, the environment, use
and priorities of the system are quite different. As a result, the software directions will be very different.

First of all, there is no need anywhere for multiprogramming. The personal computers are certainly uniprogrammed.
The disk and peripheral servers are also uniprogrammed. An
environment of uniprogrammed machines implies great changes
in the system software, especially in operating systems.
There is no need for complicated scheduling. There is no need
for elaborate process switching. There is no need for complex memory allocation. All the painstaking work and experience on complicated resource allocation algorithms in a mul-
tiprogrammed system becomes largely irrelevant. There are
many other side effects of uniprogramming in terms of security, concurrency, back-up strategies, etc. The major portion
of current centralized operating systems software is no longer
required. There is also a multiplier effect on simplification. Current operating systems resemble bridges; most of
their weight is there to support themselves.

Another direction for software in this environment is the
necessity for a flexible and easy to use user interface. The
user is now alone with his own personal computer. He does
not have direct access to system or application programmers.
In addition, he is probably not very sophisticated. This
points to a new environment of computer programming. Not
only the language but the complete set of tools at the user's
disposal, such as editors, graphics, design tools, etc.,
should be designed for ease of use. The emphasis should be
on end-user tools and not all-encompassing tools for the sophisticated programmer. In addition, we can afford to con-
sume great amounts of processing power to make this interface
friendly. Artificial Intelligence techniques which were for-
bidding in the past may now be appropriate.

ORGANIZATION COMPUTING SERVICES

Organization computing services do not seem to be affected as much by hardware changes. The investment in terms of software is so massive that changes due to hardware can only be gradually and very carefully introduced in the software. There are, however, two aspects of the system that are indirectly influenced.

First, since processing is cheaper, there can be some tradeoff between hardware and simplicity of operation. Some of the bottlenecks in the system can be eased by more hardware rather than by smarter algorithms, as was the case in the past. The net effect may be a system which is more robust. Current systems, like high performance automobiles, are very sensitive. Their simplification may make them easier to understand, to maintain and to change. Unfortunately, the optimization algorithms are an integral part of the systems as they currently exist. It will be very difficult to take them out. We hope that by running the systems in a less constrained environment the optimization strategies will become less important. If they are not used as often, they will eventually migrate to parts of the system where they can naturally wither away.

A second, indirect influence on organization computing services will be provided by the unbundling of personal computing services. The net effect will be less terminal support and fewer interrupts. The main cost of personal services is not so much actual computing services provided to the end user, but the system overhead required to maintain a dialog with the end user. When this dialog is eliminated or reduced, the central systems providing organization services can concentrate more on large programs. They can probably run with lower levels of multiprogramming and do task switching less frequently. At least they will not have to deal with real-time constraints associated with users waiting in front of terminals. As a matter of fact, the on-line operations of these systems can be factored out completely. Personal on-line services can be provided by independent personal computers. The rest of the on-line activity is mainly interaction

services through a common data base. Suppose these services
are factored out too as we will see in the next section. Then
the only jobs remaining in the central system will be what are
currently called background jobs. If we allow these jobs to
come into the foreground, it will eliminate most of the
bottlenecks in any computer center. In addition, we can
expand the hardware base to give them ample processing power
and ample real memory. They should run better and faster.
Finally, the computer center personnel can concentrate on
these important organization jobs rather than trying to answer arbitrary requests and associated phone calls from all
sorts of users.

In summary, cheaper hardware and the absence of personal
computing services and possibly interaction services will
enable centralized organization computing services to run more
smoothly. They will provide fewer functions to fewer customers in a less constrained environment. They can afford to
run a simple operation with a few well defined goals.

INTERACTION SERVICES

With the separation of personal and organization computing
services, interaction services become especially important.
They provide the means for coordination and control of the
entire system. In addition, they provide the common link not
only between people individually, but between people and the
organization as a whole.

There are two types of interaction. In the first, which
we call *limited interaction*, we are interested in communicating to a few people some information with limited scope and
short range importance. We do not expect this information to
be relevant, or even understood, by many people. We also
expect most of the material communicated to become quickly
obsolete. Therefore, we need a message system which can
route messages to appropriate destinations.

In the second case, which we will call *global interaction*,
we want to broadcast, widely, information that is relevant to
many and may have long range importance. In this case, we
would like to use a common data base which is accessible by

many people and which retains the information for further use. We do not claim that limited interaction can only be provided by message systems. It can also be provided (and it has been provided in the past) by data bases with appropriate access restrictions. In addition, global interaction can be provided, in principle, with message systems that can broadcast messages widely. Our point is that we may need both message systems and data base systems for the different aspects of interaction.

Both of these two kinds of systems introduce some very interesting software problems. In the case of an interaction-oriented data base service, the common information base is provided by one or more systems with a large amount of storage. These systems are not file servers, like the ones needed in personal computing services. That is, they do not provide just space to store data. Such a limited service defeats the goal of interaction through a common information base. The interaction-oriented data base systems should be designed to process a large number of transactions from different users exchanging information through a common data base. The stream of transactions is arbitrary and does not progress in an orderly fashion through the data base. This situation implies a rather sophisticated system which can handle many independent transactions in a real-time environment.

It is not clear whether these systems will be better provided by special purpose data base machines. They may very well be provided by general purpose processors. However, we expect these systems to be separate from the systems providing organization computing services. Many general computer systems make the distinction currently in time by running transactions during the day and large organization services at night. In the future this distinction may be reinforced by providing different systems and passing parts of the data base between them. This type of operation will allow each system to operate in a stable environment. We propose, in fact, that the batch-oriented data base activity and the transaction-oriented data base activity be separate. This may seem radical but the only link between the services is the common data base. This link can be preserved by having two systems which have access to the same final repository of data.

In the case of interaction-oriented message systems, there is a huge discrepancy between what a message system needs and what network protocols provide. High-level protocols for the free and quick exchange of messages should be developed. They need to ship not only files but transactions as messages, forms as messages, answers as messages, letters as messages, etc. Application-oriented message systems are also needed. Switching of messages should be uniform and independent of the desired destination (be that another personal computer, a data base system, etc.). These systems should make all the peculiarities of the actual networks used transparent (whether they are broadcasting networks, satellite communications, packet switching, etc.).

We have discussed limited and global interaction separately as if they were independent of each other. As a matter of fact, they are not. There is a natural transition where some of the information that is treated as a limited interaction becomes globally relevant and important and should be treated as a global interaction. If message systems offer limited interaction and data base systems offer global interaction, then there should be a natural connection among them. They should not be developed in isolation. Information should be able to migrate easily between message systems and data base systems. The migration of information implies some common models and, perhaps, complicated translation algorithms.

The second connection is between global interaction services and organization computing services. The organization services operate on data provided by the global interaction services. This was the case in the past where data base systems had a batch operation aspect and an on-line transaction aspect. This cooperation should be preserved even if the data base transaction aspects are separated from the organization computing services.

CONCLUDING REMARKS

Technology is changing fast. Perhaps the shape of components is the same but their cost is quite different. This situation influences very much the overall system architecture, function, and utilization of computers. We expect computer systems to evolve in the following directions:

1) Personal computers with clusters of peripheral servers to provide personal computing services with emphasis on ease of use.

2) Large centralized systems running in a simplified manner to provide organization computing services.

3) Message systems that provide an environment for limited interaction.

4) Transaction-oriented data base systems providing global interaction with connection to both organization services and message systems.

If we accept the foregoing, then there will be some major changes in terms of software directions:

1) There will be a need for end user tools in personal computing services as opposed to systems tools, e.g., systems programming languages.

2) Some traditional areas of software engineering, e.g., multiprogramming, dynamic resource allocation, scheduling, process switching, etc., will become less important since we will mainly operate in a uniprogramming environment.

3) Transaction-oriented data base systems will become extremely important as a common link between personal, organization and interaction services.

4) Message systems will be needed which provide a uniform interaction tool irrespective of network characteristics and which will be able to interface readily with data base systems.

The major shift, in our opinion, can be summarized by the motto "trade hardware for simplicity". For a long time we have been trying to develop techniques and methodologies for dealing with complexity. We have had partial success in doing so. However, the application of all these techniques is not easy. Perhaps we should acknowledge that computer scientists are no more intelligent and creative than other scientists. Rather than always trying to deal with complexity, we should try to remove some of it. Hardware is getting cheaper. We can sacrifice some of this good fortune to make our systems simpler and our lives easier.

SOFTWARE MUST EVOLVE

Earl C. Van Horn

Digital Equipment Corporation
Maynard, Massachusetts

INTRODUCTION

There is a tendency to think of a computer program as
something static -- something that does not change once it
correctly implements an intended function. In practice, however, programs are seldom static, particularly those that are
large and complex enough to be called software systems. As
long as a software system is used, one can expect a continual
flow of requests for its modification. Belady and Lehman
(1976) have codified this observation in their Law of Continuing Change:

> *"A system that is used undergoes continuing*
> *change until it is judged more cost effec-*
> *tive to freeze and re-create it."*

Moreover, the continual modification of a system often reduces its capacity to undergo further modification, so that
the day of freezing and re-creating arrives sooner rather than
later. The same authors have codified this phenomenon in
their Law of Increasing Entropy:

> *"The entropy of a system (its unstruc-*
> *turedness) increases with time, unless*
> *specific work is executed to maintain*
> *or reduce it."*

The re-creation of an existing system is always risky and
costly. The old system must remain in service, often for
years, while the new one is being created. If the old system

continues to be modified, the new one may be less satisfactory
than the old in some respects. If the old system is not modified, users may have to forego needed changes until the new
system is installed. When the new system is installed, errors
may be found in functions the old system performed correctly.
Although none of these problems are theoretically necessary,
their prevention is costly.

Is re-creation necessary? One way to avoid it would be to
repeal the Law of Continuing Change. It might be argued that
if our techniques for requirements analysis, design, and validation were only good enough, we would be able to get a software system right the first time, and not have to put up with
continuing change. I do not believe this will happen very
frequently in the foreseeable future, and in any case we cannot afford to wait. We must learn to live with the Law of
Continuing Change.

Perhaps we can still avoid re-creation. If somehow we
could learn to evolve systems rather than periodically re-
create them, we could avoid the trauma of re-creation, or at
least experience it less frequently.

There is hope that this evolutionary approach will suc-
ceed, because software evolution, i.e., the modification of
existing software, has not received the research and engineering effort it deserves. I shall attempt to explain why software evolution has received so little attention, and shall
mention some ways to aid and improve it. One way is to avoid
the inappropriate connotations of the word "maintenance",
which I am doing here by using the word "evolution". I want
to encourage acceptance of evolution as the normal mode of
software engineering, and encourage development of methods
and tools for evolution.

A CRITIQUE OF "MAINTENANCE"

Maintenance Has Been Neglected

An important aspect of software engineering is concern for
maintenance costs, that is, the costs of modifying a software
product after it is placed in service. Maintenance costs can

be a large fraction of the total cost of a software product, often larger than all other development costs combined [Boehm (1976); and Munson (1978)].

Nevertheless, little attention has been given to methods and tools for maintenance itself. Maintenance tends to be addressed indirectly, by creating better methods and tools for the other aspects of software development. To be specific, Figure 1 shows the typical stages in the sequential model of software development. All the activities in Figure 1 except maintenance have received considerable study, and the available literature reflects this. For example:

o   Most of the January 1977 issue of the *IEEE Transactions on Software Engineering* is devoted to requirements analysis. Formal languages, many of them processed by computer, are being developed to describe and analyze requirements [Teichroew and Hershey (1977); Ross (1977); Alford (1978); and Lamb et al. (1978)].

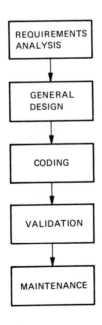

FIGURE 1. Sequential software development.

o   Various methodologies and criteria for general
    design have been explained [Parnas (1972, 1979);
    Myers (1975); Jackson (1975); and White and
    Booth (1976)], and there are computer systems
    for describing and analyzing designs [Riddle
    et al. (1978); Hammond, Murphy, and Smith
    (1978); and Boyd and Pizzarello (1978)].

o   There is advice on how to code for understand-
    ability [Kernighan and Plauger (1974)]. We
    are also encouraged to practice structured cod-
    ing [Dijkstra (1968)] and told of the benefits
    of top-down programming, chief programmer teams,
    and the like [Mills (1975); Baker (1972); and
    Brooks (1975)].

o   Validation includes both testing and verifica-
    tion. There are techniques for test case gen-
    eration [Goodenough and Gerhart (1975); Clarke
    (1976); and Ramamoorthy, Ho, and Chen (1976)],
    symbolic execution [King (1975); Boyer, Elspas,
    and Levitt (1975); and Clarke (1976)], auto-
    mated test execution [Panzl (1978)], informal
    inspections [Fagan (1974); and Yourdon (1977)],
    and formal proofs of correctness [Gries (1976);
    and Good, London, and Bledsoe (1975)].

In contrast to the other topics listed in Figure 1, there
is not a lot of literature on maintenance [Boehm (1976)].
What little there is tends to be descriptive rather than constructive, i.e., it discusses maintenance and how to manage
it, but not methods and tools for actually doing maintenance
[Munson (1978); and Swanson (1976)].

Why has maintenance been neglected? Maintenance costs
are acknowledged to be important, and researchers justify
their projects by saying that maintenance costs will be reduced, but few are eager to study maintenance directly.

What is Maintenance?

To understand the neglect of maintenance, let us first
understand what maintenance is. In an analysis slightly different from that of Swanson (1976), maintenance has four

purposes:

Correction

Adaptation

Enhancement

Restructuring

Correction is modification to fix bugs, that is, to make the software function as intended. Whether or not the intended function is specified in writing, correction involves only conformity to that function. It has nothing to do with whether the intended function meets the client's real needs.

Adaptation is modification because of a change in supporting hardware or software. For example, if a file access entry in an operating system has been changed to return more error codes, modification to recognize the new codes would be adaptive maintenance. For another example, a decision to standardize on a particular data base management package would initiate adaptive maintenance in those applications not currently using the package. Ideally, adaptive maintenance should not affect user interfaces.

A large fraction of what is considered maintenance in many organizations is enchancement, which is modification to meet new or unrecognized user requirements. Enhancement can be as simple as a change in a tax rate, or as complex as the installation of a sub-system to monitor the progress of orders in a factory.

Finally, maintenance can be done to restructure the software, i.e., to improve its internal structure while preserving its external behavior. One reason for restructuring is to make the current function easier to validate; for example, one might rewrite an operating system's kernel so that it can be proved secure. Restructuring can also make a system more understandable, and hence easier to maintain in the future.

What's in the Word "Maintenance"?

All software maintenance is done for one or more of the foregoing purposes, but no such activity is really maintenance. In standard English, "maintenance" means to restore something to its original, satisfactory condition, but that

is not the objective of software maintenance [Mills (1976);
and Munson (1978)]. Unlike spark plugs or house paint, software does not wear out. Consequently, software maintenance
is never restorative, but is always aimed at producing something better than the original.

Software maintenance is in fact engineering, i.e., re-
engineering of an existing product for one of the four purposes mentioned above. If the person who maintains your
television set were to do the kind of "maintenance" that software maintainers do, he would be able to re-design the circuitry to correct an interference problem or add a split
screen capability for viewing two channels at once.

The fact that software "maintenance" is not really maintenance is not in itself a serious problem. It simply means
that the term "maintenance" is jargon for the modification of
software already in service. Jargon is common in technical
fields; if everybody knows what a term means, there should be
no difficulty. In fact, most software people do understand
that software maintenance is the activity explained in the
preceding section.

But that is not the whole story. Although software people have dropped the standard denotation of "maintenance",
they generally have retained its connotations. In English,
"maintenance" connotes an activity that requires relatively
less skill than the design of the object being maintained.
For example, it takes a roomful of people with college degrees to design a television set, but one can learn to maintain a television set by taking a correspondence course. By
connotation, a "maintenance man" is someone with relatively
low skill, relatively low pay, and relatively low prestige.
Of course, there is no reason why maintenance work is necessarily low in skill, pay, or prestige; for example, physicians
are basically maintenance men for the human body. Nevertheless, the word does have those connotations.

THE IMPORTANCE OF SOFTWARE EVOLUTION

In order to avoid the inappropriate negative connotations
of the word "maintenance", I shall instead use the word "evolution" to refer to the modification of existing software
[Belady and Lehman (1976); and Belady (1979)]. It is easy to
accept the idea that software evolution is important, challenging and rewarding -- certainly more so than mere maintenance.

The Growth of Code in Service

Today, software evolution is economically the most important aspect of software development. As mentioned previously,
the cost of evolving a system after it is in service is
typically greater than all other life-cycle costs combined.
I suspect the majority of programmers are employed to evolve
software already in service, and no doubt a comparable portion of development computer resources are used for such
evolution. Furthermore, evolution can be expected to become
more important in the future, because the amount of code
available for evolution will increase as new programs are
placed in service faster than old ones are retired [Boehm
(1976)].

In the future, however, software evolution will be even
more important than the growth of code in service might indicate, because it is becoming more difficult for the first
release of a system to meet all of a client's needs. There
are two reasons for this.

The Growth of Functional Complexity

First, software systems are becoming more complex, because computer hardware is becoming faster and cheaper, and
because clients are demanding more functions, better interfaces, and more fault tolerance. This increasing complexity
will continually challenge the technology of software creation, so we must recognize that even our most sophisticated
techniques for design, coding, and validation may not be equal
to the task of getting a system right on the first try. We

must be prepared to develop a system in stages, all but the
first of which is an evolution of its predecessor [Basili and
Turner (1975)].

Creation of new software in stages is done today; the
stages are sometimes called base levels. Each base level is
both a technical and a management checkpoint. It proves fea-
sibility of a portion of the design, and provides meaningful
measurement of progress in an activity that is notoriously
difficult to measure. Thus even the creation of new software
can best be treated as an evolutionary process, and the increasing complexity of applications will force us to rely on
this technique more.

The Evolution of Client Needs

There is a second, more fundamental reason why it is difficult to meet all a client's needs on the first try. Even
if we were able to meet a client's initially perceived requirements correctly (perhaps by evolution through base
levels), a client's first set of requirements is seldom his
ultimate.

Consequently, a new and complex computer application must
be developed in stages that the client can use and react to.
At the beginning of this process, the client will undoubtedly
understand his needs in terms of the automation of today's
manual activities. Once that automation exists, the client's
work flow, division of labor, costs, and even his products or
services will change as a result of the new tool. In this
new environment he will perceive further needs, and these will
lead to changes and additions to his computer tool, which will
in turn give rise to another environment, etc.

The most advanced requirements analysis technique cannot
be relied on to discover the client's ultimate computer tool,
because the client himself usually has no conception of this
tool. Even if the requirements analyst has enough application
knowledge to be able to imagine the ultimate tool, the proposal for it would no doubt be impossible to sell, because
it would be so far from the client's experience.

Because of the complex interaction between a client's
needs and his computer tools, and because it is usually too

costly to create a new software system every time a client
perceives new needs, the software for a new and complex application must evolve as the client's perception of his needs
evolves.

Notice how the connotations of the word "maintenance"
could be misleading if applied to the above activities. Maintenance (in the English sense) is necessary only because our
physical products are not perfect. If a product is made of
better materials or designed for longer service, it will require less maintenance. Maintenance is a necessary anomaly
-- something one should not have to do.

How wrong it would be to conclude that software evolution
is something one should not have to do. Evolution -- née
maintenance -- is a fundamental technique of software engineering. It is potent for managing complexity, and essential
for helping clients understand their needs.

SOFTWARE EVOLUTION TODAY

Nevertheless, the practice of software evolution leaves
much to be desired. As mentioned in the discussion of "maintenance", there has been little research on evolution itself.
There is lots of advice on how to design evolvable software,
but little on how to actually do evolution.

Most of the tools available to evolvers are hand-me-downs
from software creators. Although programming library systems
are becoming more popular [Baker (1975); Glasser (1978); and
Bauer and Birchall (1978)], and cross-references of linker
symbols are common enough, there is rarely a system cross-
reference that contains the names of include files and macros,
for example. Information retrieval technology has not been
vigorously applied to the problem of obtaining information
about the structure, code, and documentation of an existing
software system. Yet the quality of software evolution depends critically on how well the evolver understands the system he is evolving. We are not doing everything we could to
facilitate that understanding.

Perhaps because of the negative connotations of "maintenance", software evolution is not well rewarded. It is not

well paid, nor is it considered challenging or prestigious.
Junior programmers are assigned to do evolution, partly because it is believed that a low skill level is required, and
partly because senior programmers want to do creation and will
change employers rather than do "maintenance".

Creation is considered to be where the action is. For
example, I know an environmental technology firm that had
trouble hiring good programmers to evolve their software. But
when the firm decided to create a replacement for one of their
systems, they had no trouble hiring good people to do that.
One factor in the decision to undertake a creation project
was that it seemed the only way to attract better programmers
into the organization.

There is something like a Peter Principle [Peter and Hull
(1970)] at work in software evolution. Once a programmer has
become skilled at evolution, or even at evolving a particular
system, he moves to the next creation project that comes
along, leaving new people and marginal performers to tend to
the evolution of existing systems.

With all these negative factors at work, is it any wonder
that software evolution today is so costly and problematical?

SOFTWARE EVOLUTION TOMORROW

Evolvability as a Goal of Evolution

One way of improving software evolution is to use evolvability as a design criterion, and thus develop systems whose
structure facilitates their evolution. Many current techniques, such as information hiding [Parnas (1972)], minimiza-
tion of interfaces [Myers (1975)], and structured coding
[Dijkstra (1968)], do make evolution easier, but they are
applied mostly during software creation, and not often during
evolution.

It is not enough merely to create evolvable software; we
must preserve evolvability during evolution. In order to do
this we must have the courage to restructure a system when
the old structure is inappropriate. For example, if a new
command language construct is best handled by providing an

extra parameter to the lexical analyzer, we must make that
change, even though it means changing and re-validating a
dozen existing calls.

Software evolvers today are often under pressure to make
changes quickly and with minimum risk to existing functions.
Unfortunately these goals conflict with that of preserving
evolvability by restructuring. Not every change will require
restructuring, but when evolvers say that restructuring is
necessary, they must be allowed to do it. Management must
understand that an occasional delay in delivery of a change,
and an occasional error introduced because of restructuring,
are preferable to having patches accumulate like barnacles
until excessive delay and risk accompany every change and a
totally new system must be created. If occasional small delays and risks are accepted to preserve evolvability, the
life of a system will be extended, perhaps indefinitely.

Once the techniques of evolution are in use, we can do
more than simply preserve evolvability. If we know what
constitutes an evolvable structure, and if we have the methods
and tools to restructure a system, we can actually improve a
system, i.e., we can evolve it so as to improve its evolvability. For example, if a system's data base manager and
output spooler each has its own queue handler, the handlers
could be replaced by a single queue handler. The common
handler is more likely to be usable by the message dispatcher
that will be added next year, and any queue handling improvements can be made and validated only once.

If evolvability can be improved by evolution, we need not
be so concerned with having the very best structure when the
software is created. Any flaws in structure can be healed as
the software evolves.

Attitudes and Training for Evolution

As mentioned above, software creation is now considered
to be where the action is, and to offer challenge, prestige,
and rewards. Evolution is considered a necessary anomaly to
correct deficiencies of creation. I advocate a reversal of
our attitudes toward these two activities. Software evolution
should be considered to be where the action is, and to offer

challenge, prestige, and rewards. Creation should be considered a necessary anomaly to get the evolutionary process
started.

It may take several years for this change of attitudes to
occur, but it must occur. Evolution is too important to be
left to junior people; it requires the best programmers available. In a large system with complex parts and interactions,
there are often many ways in which a change can be made.
Choosing the right way requires knowledge of the system, skill
in applying design criteria, and judgment to know when a restructuring must be done. Furthermore, because the system is
in service, the evolver has a great responsibility: the work
must be done correctly and must not disrupt current operations.

There is, of course, no better place for on-the-job training than the crucible of evolution. But a newcomer should not
evolve alone. Evolution should be done by a senior and junior
person working as a team. The senior has responsibility and
teaches, while the junior accepts assignments and learns.
When the junior has learned enough, he can take a tour of duty
in creation, where he has a chance to try out some design
principles and gain a greater appreciation for trade-offs.
Later he will return to evolution, this time as a senior person giving guidance to yet another newcomer.

Tools for Evolution

Emphasis on evolution should yield better tools to support
it. Software development, which consists of both creation and
evolution, should be considered a computer application just
like banking or process control. Its requirements should be
analyzed, and maximum feasible computer power should be applied to support it. The resulting support system should use
the best information retrieval technology to help developers
understand the system being developed. For example, a support
system could:

(a) Provide interactive browsing in code and documenta-
     tion, with the aid of cross-reference information,

(b) Display only the kind of information desired, such
     as procedure headings but not procedure bodies,

(c) Draw diagrams showing the high-level structure of
     the system, providing additional detail as requested,

(d) Provide a graphical, interactive design language, in
     which the design is related to the code, and

(e) Keep track of the changes made by different program-
     mers at different times.

A support system for evolution would include many features
of current integrated development approaches [Dolotta and
Mashey (1976); Davis and Vick (1978); Osterweil, Brown, and
Stucki (1978); Bratman and Court (1975); and Irvine and
Brackett (1977)]. More details of what such a system would
be like may be found in proposals for one called SEER [Van
Horn (1978)] and for one being developed at the University of
Connecticut [White and Booth (1979)].

The Evolutionary Development Process

In a world in which evolution is considered the normal
mode of software development, one will seldom see the development process diagrammed as in Figure 1. Instead, the process
will be thought of in terms of the evolutionary model shown
in Figure 2. Each interval of implementation is followed by
engineering evaluation for such factors as correctness, performance, and quality of design. The product will be returned
to implementation if it is unsatisfactory or if it is only a
base level.

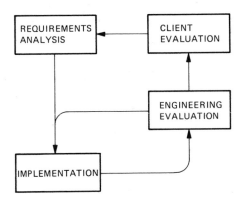

FIGURE 2. Evolutionary Software Development.

If a product passes the engineering evaluation, it is placed in service for the client. His evaluation is input to a requirements analysis activity, which will define the requirements for subsequent implementation. For each client the development process begins in the requirements analysis phase.

The time around the client loop can be anything from a few days to a year, and there may be several developments proceeding around the loop at different rates. An important function of a development support system is to help control multiple asynchronous developments. The time around the engineering loop may be as short as a day or two, but base levels should be introduced if necessary so that the engineering loop does not take more than a few months.

The familiar phases of general design, coding and validation can still exist, but they are details of implementation. The distinctions between them are less important than the distinctions shown in Figure 2. For example, coding and validation of a program can occur concurrently [Baker (1972); and Dijkstra (1976)].

CONCLUSION

For many years software people have bemoaned the fact that so little code is reused. But reuse is just evolution viewed from a different perspective: if software evolves, then the part that remains unchanged is reused. Methods, tools, and attitudes that favor evolution will therefore tend to encourage reuse, and so will help reduce duplication of effort.

The most precious thing in software engineering is the program whose correctness and usefulness has been confirmed by actual service [Belady (1979)]. We must learn how to preserve, reuse, and improve these jewels, and must reward those who do [Rawson (1978)].

REFERENCES

Alford, M. W. (Nov. 1978). Software requirements engineering
    methodology (SREM) at the age of two, *Proc. COMPSAC-78*,
    332-339.
Baker, F. T. (1972). Chief programmer team management of
    production programming, *IBM Systems J. 11*, 56-73.
Baker, F. T. (June 1975). Structured programming in a pro-
    duction programming environment, *IEEE Trans. Software Eng.
    SE-1*, 241-252.
Basili, V. R., and Turner, A. J. (Dec. 1975). Iterative en-
    hancement: A practical technique for software development,
    IEEE Trans. Software Eng. SE-1, 390-396.
Bauer, H. A., and Birchall, R. H. (Nov. 1978). Managing large
    scale software development with an automated change con-
    trol system, *Proc. COMPSAC-78*, 13-17.
Belady, L. A. (Feb. 1979). Evolved software for the 80's,
    Computer 12(2), 79-82.
Belady, L. A., and Lehman, M. M. (1976). A model of large
    program development, *IBM Systems J. 15(3)*, 225-252.
Boehm, B. W. (Dec. 1976). Software engineering, *IEEE Trans.
    Computers C-25*, 1226-1241.
Boyd, D. L., and Pizzarello, A. (July 1978). Introduction
    to the WELLMADE design methodology, *IEEE Trans. Software
    Eng. SE-4*, 276-282.
Boyer, R. S., Elspas, B., and Levitt, K. N. (June 1975).
    SELECT -- A formal system for testing and debugging pro-
    grams by symbolic execution, *Proc. 1975 Int. Conf. Reli-
    able Software, ACM SIGPLAN Notices 10*, 234-245.
Bratman, H., and Court, T. (May 1975). The software factory,
    Computer 8(5), 28-37.
Brooks, F. P. (1975). "The Mythical Man-Month," Reading,
    Mass.: Addison-Wesley.
Clarke, L. A. (Sept. 1976). A system to generate test data
    and symbolically execute programs, *IEEE Trans. Software
    Eng. SE-2*, 215-222.
Davis, C. G., and Vick, C. R. (Nov. 1978). The software de-
    velopment system: Status and evolution, *Proc. COMPSAC-78*,
    326-331.

Dijkstra, E. W. (March 1968). Go to statement considered harmful, *Commun. Assoc. Comput. Mach. 11*, 147–148.

Dijkstra, E. W. (1976). "A Discipline of Programming," Englewood Cliffs, N.J.: Prentice-Hall.

Dolotta, T. A., and Mashey, J. R. (Oct. 1976). An introduction to the programmer's workbench, *Proc. Second Int. Conf. Software Eng.*, 164–168.

Fagan, M. E. (Dec. 1974). "Design and Code Inspections and Process Control in the Development of Programs," Rep. TR 21.572, IBM System Dev. Div., Kingston, NY.

Glasser, A. L. (Nov. 1978). The evolution of a source code control system, *Proc. Software Quality and Assurance Workshop, Software Engineering Notes 3(5)*, 122–125.

Good, D. I., London, R. L., and Bledsoe, W. W. (March 1975). An interactive program verification system, *IEEE Trans. Software Eng. SE-1*, 59–67.

Goodenough, J. B., and Gerhart, S. L. (June 1975). Toward a theory of test data selection, *IEEE Trans. Software Eng. SE-1*, 156–173.

Gries, D. (Dec. 1976). An illustration of current ideas on the derivation of correctness proofs and correct programs, *IEEE Trans. Software Eng. SE-2*, 238–244.

Hammond, L. S., Murphy, D. L., and Smith, M. K. (Nov. 1978). A system for analysis and verification of a software design, *Proc. COMPSAC-78*, 42–47.

Irvine, C. A., and Brackett, J. W. (Jan. 1977). Automated software engineering through structured data management, *IEEE Trans. Software Eng. SE-3*, 34–40.

Jackson, M. A. (1975). "Principles of Program Design," New York: Academic Press.

Kernighan, B. W., and Plauger, P. J. (1974). "The Elements of Programming Style," New York: McGraw-Hill.

King, J. C. (June 1975). A new approach to program testing, *Proc. 1975 Int. Conf. Reliable Software, ACM SIGPLAN Notices 10*, 228–233.

Lamb, S. S., et al. (Nov. 1978). SAMM: A modeling tool for requirements and design specification, *Proc. COMPSAC-78*, 48–53.

Mills, H. D. (June 1975). How to write correct programs and
    know it, *Proc. 1975 Int. Conf. Reliable Software, ACM
    SIGPLAN Notices 10*, 363-370.

Mills, H. D. (Dec. 1976). Software development, *IEEE Trans.
    Software Eng. SE-2*, 265-273.

Munson, J. B. (Nov. 1978). Software maintainability: A
    practical concern for life-cycle costs, *Proc. COMPSAC-78*,
    54-59.

Myers, G. L. (1975). "Reliable Software Through Composite
    Design," New York: Petrocelli/Charter.

Osterweil, L. J., Brown, J. R., and Stucki, L. G. (Nov. 1978).
    ASSET, A lifecycle verification and visibility system,
    Proc. COMPSAC-78, 30-35.

Panzl, D. J. (May 1978). Automatic revision of formal test
    procedures, *Proc. Third Int. Conf. Software Eng.*, 320-326.

Parnas, D. L. (Dec. 1972). On the criteria to be used in de-
    composing systems into modules, *Commun. Assoc. Comput.
    Mach. 15*, 1053-1058.

Parnas, D. L. (March 1979). Designing software for ease of
    extension and contraction, *IEEE Trans. Software Eng. SE-5*,
    128-138.

Peter, L. J., and Hull, R. (1970). "The Peter Principle,"
    New York: Bantam.

Ramamoorthy, C. V., Ho, Siv-Bun F., and Chen, W. T. (Dec.
    1976). On the automated generation of program test data,
    IEEE Trans. Software Eng. SE-2, 293-300.

Rawson, E. B. (Feb. 1978). Standard software modules: Can
    we find the pot of gold?, *Digest of Papers COMPCON Spring
    78*, 285-287.

Riddle, W. E., et al. (July 1978). Behavior modeling during
    software design, *IEEE Trans. Software Eng. SE-4*, 283-292.

Ross, D. T. (Jan. 1977). Structured analysis (SA): A lan-
    guage for communicating ideas, *IEEE Trans. Software Eng.
    SE-3*, 16-34.

Swanson, E. B. (Oct. 1976). The dimensions of maintenance,
    Proc. Second Int. Conf. Software Eng., 492-497.

Teichroew, D., and Hershey, E. A. (Jan. 1977). PSL/PSA: A
    computer-aided technique for structured documentation and
    analysis of information processing systems, *IEEE Trans.
    Software Eng. SE-3*, 41-48.

Van Horn, E. C. (Nov. 1978). Software evolution using the
    SEER data base, *Proc. COMPSAC-78*, 147-152.
White, J. R., and Booth, T. L. (Oct. 1976). Towards an engi-
    neering approach to software design, *Proc. Second Int.
    Conf. Software Eng.*, 214-222.
White, J. R., and Booth, T. L. (July 1979). "Research in
    Advanced Support Systems for Software Development and
    Maintenance," Rep. CS-79-11, U. Conn. Computer Sci. Div.,
    Storrs, Conn.
Yourdon, E. (1977). "Structured Walkthroughs," New York:
    Yourdon.

SOFTWARE DEVELOPMENT -
THERE'S GOT TO BE A BETTER WAY!

John F. Wassenberg

Norden Systems
Norwalk, Connecticut

INTRODUCTION

In spite of dramatic increases in computer hardware technology, the software engineering capability required to use
this technology most effectively has not kept pace. In fact,
it is doubtful that under current software engineering procedures, the truly effective use of computer technology in some
functional areas will not be achieved in the foreseeable future. This is particularly true for computer systems which
support military electronic systems requirements. The requirements of these embedded computer systems, as they are
called, are usually pushing the available software technology.
This is caused by increasing threats due to the rapidly emerg-
ing weapons systems hardware technologies. This produces a
"Catch-22" situation. New technology provides new weapons
systems capabilities which require even newer technology to
counter these capabilities. In addition, more and more of
these new weapons systems are computer supported and computer
dependent. This situation produces significant side effects
which further compound the software development problem. As
threats are identified or even perceived, the need to counter
these threats becomes time sensitive. This leads to hurriedly
and usually inadequately defined requirements accompanied by
unrealistic need dates usually resulting in unattainable
schedules. On the other hand, the fact that most computer
supported military electronic systems progress through normally excessively long program initiation, demonstration and

validation, and full-scale engineering development phases before becoming operational, almost ensures that such systems
will be at least obsolescent by the time they become operational.

Software has become and will continue to be a pacing factor in computer supported military systems acquisition.
Unless better ways are found soon to support more effectively
the software development for these systems, the situation can
only get worse.

PROBLEMS STILL ABOUND

The development of software as part of the acquisition of
computer-supported military systems is still frought with
problems -- in spite of over 20 years of experience in this
area. Actual costs continue to exceed estimates. Late de-
liveries are commonplace. Demonstrated performance often
does not meet operational requirements. Software errors continue to appear and software reliability is questionable.
Inadequate documentation makes software maintenance difficult
if not impossible.

Since these are continually recurring problems, one would
think solutions would be well in hand. Actual practice seems
to indicate the contrary. Software productivity levels remain low in spite of significant efforts to improve them. It
seems we are destined to continue to face the same problems
as our predecessors, unless a better way can be found to develop software.

An analysis of the observable manifestations of the software problems as indicated above leads to a better understanding of the underlying causes of these problems. Some of the
principal causes can be summarized as follows:

Lack of early management visibility.
Lack of software management discipline.
Lack of life cycle perspective.
Lack of adequate software requirements and risk analysis.
Lack of adequate software resource estimating procedures.
Lack of adequate milestone definition and acceptance
    criteria.

Lack of standards and inability to enforce standards.
Difficulty in transfer of software engineering technology.
Uncoordinated software research and development.

It is readily apparent that the root causes are primarily
management and technical in nature. Therefore, the solutions
have to come from better management procedures and improved
software engineering technology. From a systems viewpoint,
these are not and cannot be independent solutions. However,
it is a lack of understanding of the software development
process that leads to most of the management problems. One
would expect that part of the solution lies in a better in-
formed management as to the software development process and
that this should lead to the development of the management
disciplines so sorely needed. On the other hand, a more en-
lightened management would probably recognize the need for
increased software technology transfer and support the efforts
required to achieve it. This should result in improvements
in software engineering methodology and in software development. However, there is still a continued reluctance on the
part of many software engineers to fully appreciate the true
"support" nature of their role in the acquisition of computer-
supported systems. This may, in fact, be the most prevalent
reason for the majority of the identified software problems.

SOLUTIONS ARE HARD TO FIND

Certainly no one intimately associated with computer-
supported systems expects the software development process to
be easy. But one could have expected that lessons learned
would have identified practical and cost effective solutions.
Yet there appears to be little significant change in the way
we develop software now than how we did in the past. Surely
the advent of high order languages, structured programming,
top down design, programming, and test have made the software
engineer's task easier. Perhaps, but more likely these advances in software engineering techniques and tools have more
than been offset by the increases in computer hardware capabilities and the need for the more complex software to meet
today's even more complex requirements. Much could be said

for the fact that what is perceived as new software technology
is really the recognition and formalization of techniques and
technology that many independent software engineering activities had long been using. Again, it was the very nature of
the software development process that almost assured that
common solutions to the software development problem would
not be found. This had to do with the early lack of software
provided by the computer manufacturers. This meant that activities acquiring a computer usually developed their own
software, primarily applications software, but often operating
systems or executive software too. The lack of an established
engineering base for software development meant it was everyone for himself. The results were predictable: little or no
standardization, a Tower of Babel as far as programming languages went, and a lack of system level or life cycle perspectives by most software engineers and programmers.

It has been only within the past few years that the
Department of Defense fully recognized the problems associated
with software development and started taking positive action
to address them. These included specific guidance and requirements for computer resource management, which included
software development. This was followed by a language standardization directive which required all new major defense
systems to be programmed in an approved high order language.
The seven approved high order languages were also specified.
A fully coordinated DOD (Army, Navy, Air Force) software
technology program was developed to provide standardized software development tools, automated development aids, and a
common high order language. In spite of some initial opposi-
tion, the Armed Services are gradually accepting the fact that
such actions are mandatory if software development, including
the cost thereof, in support of military systems is to be controlled effectively. The same can not be said for industry.
Except when DOD directs certain standards to be used, the competitive advantage in winning contracts may rest on a company's
proprietary software development tools and technology.

A prospective solution with great potential is better use
of our academic institutions. The use of computers is wide-
spread throughout academia. However their orientation and

use is almost unique to their environment. One has but to
look at available curricula and associated texts used in con-
temporary computer science courses to gain insight as to why
they contribute little to the software development problems
facing industry. The same can be said for the majority of
system engineering courses. It is little wonder then, that
only through extensive on-the-job training can the required
management and technical skills be acquired. The degree to
which this is necessary is directly related to the scope of
instruction received.

Solutions also cost money; in some cases a lot of money.
This recognition was the basis for the recently promulgated
Department of Defense coordinated Software Research and Development program - a program with annual expenditures measured in the tens of millions of dollars. The program covers
everything from software life cycle management technology
through software systems design, software engineering tools
and methods, and software verification and maintenance. One
bright light is that most of the tools and techniques developed as a result of this program will most likely be made
available to industry either by directed use on selected
government contracts or through government information services.

EDUCATION AND DISCIPLINE ARE NEEDED

Software engineering as an art, science, or discipline is
still evolving. Thus we are still learning how to develop
software as we develop it. It is this feedback from the actual development process which dictates to a great degree what
is required of our educational institutions. The problem is
that for many areas of concern, particularly in support of
military weapons systems, there are no corresponding courses
of instruction. They too have to be developed or evolved over
a period of time. This is also a Catch-22 situation - if the
courses were available, probably the solutions would be in
hand. On the other hand, the requirements for software in
computer-supported systems is not only rapidly growing, but
at the same time changing as new computer hardware technology

makes available even greater capabilities and opportunities.
It may be a long time before software engineering matures to
the point that say mechanical, electrical, or chemical engineering has.

Software, however, is pervasive. As the use of computers
becomes more commonplace - the attendant software problems
become more visible. In the military systems area, a missile
is lost due to an error in the software of the guidance system. An airplane is lost because its computer-supported
flight control system didn't operate properly at a critical
time. A submarine is lost when its computer-supported iner-
tial navigation system fails due to a software failure. The
necessary command and control information never reaches its
intended recipient because the computer-supported communications switch malfunctioned due to a software error. These
are pertinent examples since every effort is made to make
these systems as dependable and reliable as possible, and the
consequences of failure are disastrous. The fact is that
these problems continue to occur - and that is the crux of
the problem.

Continuing education is required at all levels to ensure
that not only the developers of computer supported systems,
but also the users, managers, and operators have a thorough
understanding of this thing called software - a problem com-
pounded by the very intangible nature of the software product
itself.

Full acceptance of computer-supported systems is best
achieved when the nature of the software and its development
process are fully understood. As was mentioned before, computers are being used extensively in the academic environment.
Today's high school and college graduates can hardly escape
an exposure to computer supported courses of instruction, if
not direct use of computers themselves. Most have an appreciation of what a computer is, how it operates, and the software that makes it a useful tool.

There exists however, a middle and upper management generation whose education didn't include this exposure to computers, but who are now faced with the use if not the dependence upon computers for the continued operation and growth

of their company. At issue then, is how to provide this group
with enough insight into the implications of computers and
their associated software so that they can make intelligent
decisions in this regard.

Part of this insight will come through experience with
computer-supported systems themselves - usually as a result
of being faced with all the observable manifestations of software problems previously mentioned. Part will come through
recognition of the increased role that software is playing in
their business areas of interest. But most important will be
through increased communication between the software engineering staff and all levels of management. The high costs and
other problems associated with software development can not
be long ignored.

Education and engineering discipline are not as synonomous
today as perhaps they were a couple of decades ago. Yet it
is to our educational institutions which one must look to in-
still the engineering disciplines, including those dealing
with software engineering, upon which to build to meet the
needs of rapidly evolving technology. Educators must address
better the transition from the theory of the classroom to the
practical application of industry. Early recognition is
needed that a computer and its associated software is a powerful tool that is supportive of nearly every conceivable field
of endeavor. And while we need tool makers (perhaps these
are computer science majors), the real payoff is to develop
people who know how to use this wonderful - and sometimes dia-
bolic tool called a computer. Just as mathematics is a powerful tool in support of the physical sciences, the computer
appears to be a tool destined to provide literally orders of
magnitude increase in effectivity and productivity when applied to most any or every facet of academic, business, or industrial endeavor. Never before has one invention become so
persuasive, with implications so profound. Its application
seems endless, its potential unlimited, its effect on society
unestimable. One has but to look around at its many uses
today to realize how many things could not be done without
the use of a computer.

In a way, I have fallen into a trap of my own making. I
have implied that the computer (hardware) itself is all one

needs to produce such significant advances, when, in reality,
the computer is like any other tool. Until one finds a way
to use it for a particular application, it is just so much
metal, or circuitry, or what have you. Its utility is in its
application, not in its availability. What makes the computer
a useful tool is the ability to tell it what we want it to
do -- through its software or computer programs, or perhaps
nowadays, through its design (firmware), and have it do it
faster and more accurately than humanly possible. The computer is only as "smart" as the computer programmer makes it --
and therein lies the problem we have been talking about -- the
development of computer software or the related hardware
(firmware) logic.

The point to be made is that computers are generally made
to serve other than computer manufacturers' requirements. The
fact that today's computers are for the most part general-
purpose computers means that their use is limited only by the
ingenuity one has in defining or identifying uses for their
capabilities. Unfortunately, some of the identified uses,
such as computer games, detract from its appreciation as a
tool which can greatly increase available knowledge or personal productivity. On the plus side is that the ever expand-
ing personal computer market, which, while possibly oversold
as to utility for personal use, certainly has taken the black
magic out of computers and software. However, this widespread
availability of inexpensive but powerful computers leads one
to assume that either they come with universally usable software or that software development for new applications is easy.
Both are partially true. Some software packages are provided
with the computer, and most computers also provide the capability to develop new software. This leads to perhaps the
most negative aspect of personal computers -- the relatively
undisciplined approach to new software development -- perhaps
simplistic is a better word. Regardless, this lack of discipline or appreciation of the need for discipline will often
carry over into other software associations. It is difficult
to sell the fact that a good programmer can only code a few
lines of code per day for a complex real-time system when
everyone knows how easy it is to develop new software for
your home computer.

Educators must not only provide the scientific and engineering aspects of software engineering but also the underlying and necessary discipline of software development.

FIGHT FIRE WITH FIRE - AUTOMATE

The solution is inherent in the problem -- automation. Automation creates the problem and automation can help solve the problem. If one goes back and reviews the underlying causes of current software development problems, it becomes readily apparent that people are the primary contributors to these problems, followed closely by the recurrent nature of the problem.

Even an embryonic computer systems analyst would recognize these as symptoms which warrant at least consideration of automation as a solution. The truth is automation itself is probably the only realistic and feasible solution to the very problems it creates. Like most truly useful tools, automation allows one to develop additional tools which facilitate use of the primary tool itself.

Why hasn't this been recognized before? It has, and it continues to be. Unfortunately, efforts in this area are relatively uncoordinated in spite of many industry and government groups or committees which purport to address this responsibility. There really has not been the incentive to address software standardization or the development of a universally usable set of the software tools which could result in more timely and usable software, at an affordable price and providing more capability and requiring less maintenance.

The development of software tools costs money; a lot of money. The Department of Defense currently spends in excess of 30 million dollars a year for this purpose - and has little to show for the money spent. Major plans consider the development of a new high-order language, ADA (DOD 1) purportedly designed to meet the infinite variety of applications found in defense systems. Attempts have been and continue to be made in computer hardware standardization only to find that computer hardware technology is changing so rapidly as to result in obsolescence even before approval for standardization can be achieved. It is now entirely possible, however, that as a spin-off of the advancing computer hardware technology, there may emerge the vehicle for eventual hardware standardization. That is, the development and manufacture of modular computer hardware built to form, fit, and function specifications wherein the cost of at least selected modules can be reduced to a point where it is more cost effective to discard faulty modules rather than repair them. This has the effect of being able to introduce new computer hardware technology, while retaining full software compatibility and reducing drastically hardware support costs in terms of maintenance and logistics.

Standardization of hardware and its implemented instruction set would allow the development of a compatible set of support software tools whose investment could more than be amortized by increased productivity and more reliable software.

This leads to the conclusion that the only practical and cost effective solution to the automation problem is more automation. That then is where significant research and development emphasis and money is required and should be placed. This may not be a viable solution for any given company or educational institution due to the very nature and magnitude of the effort; however, collectively, it can be done and at affordable cost.

Can it happen cooperatively? Probably not! This means that probably only through government influence, if not direction, can any great progress be made in this area. Government control versus free enterprise? I firmly believe that if significant improvements can be made in software productivity and reliability by means of government developed (or subsidized) standardized software development tools, then the majority of software development activities will accept this leadership as being in their individual and collective best interests.

Implicit in this, of course, is the idea that the software development problem is so large and of such significant impact as to warrant a common effort. The loss of possible competitive advantage which might result from such a combined effort could be more than offset by genuine ingenuity in the innovative use of these tools, the increased productivity resulting from their use and the yet untapped uses of automation.

LET'S GET ON WITH IT

Software engineering is and will remain a national problem until the nation as a whole recognizes it as such. Localizing the problem to one or another aspect of industry or academia only tends to ensure that the problem will persevere. Software engineering will remain a national issue as long as industry and academia fail to recognize the need for discipline and controlled evolution, if not standardization, in the development of software. Perhaps, as the production of computer hardware approaches the demand, then the software aspect of the use of computers will be given the attention it mandates. With current predictions of software costs approaching 95% of automated systems costs, it may not be too long before this happens.

It has been estimated that the Department of Defense will spend nearly 9.8 billion dollars a year over the next five years on computer software. The impact of increasing software development productivity, even by small amounts are obvious. If overall productivity of software development can be increased by only 1%, this could result in an annual savings of over $98 million a year. If software testing can collectively be reduced by only one week a year, annual savings of $75M are possible. If coding productivity for average systems can be increased by only one instruction per day, $245 million a year can be saved. For complex or real-time systems, this amount could approach $500 million a year. Even larger savings can be expected during the operational phase of a defense system through increased software reliability.

Software development is big money, even considering only Defense systems. Small productivity increases result in significant savings. Software development costs are predominantly people costs. Only by increasing people productivity can the rising cost of software be stemmed. Education and automation are two prime candidates to achieve this productivity. Both could use significant infusions of research and development monies in these areas. The alternatives are unaffordable software and inefficiently utilized computer hardware. There has got to be a better way.

INDEX

239